CW00430479

THAILAND'S
UNDERWATER
WORLD

A Celebration of Thailand's Amazing Marine Life

THAILAND'S
UNDERWATER
WORLD

A Celebration of Thailand's Amazing Marine Life

Text by **Chris Mitchell** · Photography by **Jez Tryner**

Marshall Cavendish
Editions

© 2012 Marshall Cavendish International (Asia) Private Limited

Published by Marshall Cavendish Editions
An imprint of Marshall Cavendish International (Asia) Private Limited
A member of Times Publishing Limited

All rights reserved

No part of this publication may be reproduced, stored in a retrieval system or transmitted, in any form or by any means, electronic, mechanical, photocopying, recording or otherwise, without the prior permission of the copyright owner. Request for permission should be addressed to the Publisher, Marshall Cavendish International (Asia) Private Limited, 1 New Industrial Road, Singapore 536196. Tel: (65) 6213 9300, Fax: (65) 6285 4871. E-mail: genref@sg.marshallcavendish.com. Website: www.marshallcavendish.com/genref

The publisher makes no representation or warranties with respect to the contents of this book, and specifically disclaims any implied warranties or merchantability or fitness for any particular purpose, and shall in no events be liable for any loss of profit or any other commercial damage, including but not limited to special, incidental, consequential, or other damages.

Other Marshall Cavendish Offices
Marshall Cavendish International. PO Box 65829, London EC1P 1NY, UK • Marshall Cavendish Corporation. 99 White Plains Road, Tarrytown NY 10591-9001, USA • Marshall Cavendish International (Thailand) Co Ltd. 253 Asoke, 12th Flr, Sukhumvit 21 Road, Klongtoey Nua, Wattana, Bangkok 10110, Thailand • Marshall Cavendish (Malaysia) Sdn Bhd, Times Subang, Lot 46, Subang Hi-Tech Industrial Park, Batu Tiga, 40000 Shah Alam, Selangor Darul Ehsan, Malaysia.

Marshall Cavendish is a trademark of Times Publishing Limited

National Library Board Singapore Cataloguing in Publication Data
Mitchell, Chris, 1972-
Thailand's underwater world : a celebration of Thailand's amazing marine life / text by Chris Mitchell ; photography by Jez Tryner. – Singapore : Marshall Cavendish Editions, c2011.
p. cm.
Includes bibliographical references.
ISBN : 978-981-4302-55-5
1. Marine animals – Thailand. 2. Marine animals – Thailand – Pictorial works. 3. Deep diving – Thailand. I. Tryner, Jez, 1969-
II. Title.
QL121
591.7709593 — dc22   OCN707597300

Editors: Greg Lowe (Thailand), Justin Lau (Singapore)
Designers: Mark Soo (Thailand), Bernard Go (Singapore)
All photos by Jez Tryner except pages 30, 149–155 by Ayesha Cantrell

Printed in Singapore by Fabulous Printers Pte Ltd

Contents

Preface

Chris Mitchell

"

FOR MANY PEOPLE, WHATEVER THEIR NATIONALITY,
THAILAND IS WHERE THEY FIRST TRULY FALL IN LOVE
WITH THE OCEAN. I KNOW THAT'S WHAT HAPPENED
TO ME.

"

Wow. That's pretty much the first thing anyone says when they see my friend Jez Tryner's underwater photos of Thailand.

It was certainly pretty much the first thing I said when I met him five years ago on the Thai island of Koh Lanta. As a field editor for *Scuba Diver AustralAsia* magazine, I'm always looking for underwater photographers to work with who can take photos not only of what there is to physically see under the ocean's surface, but also to capture something of the atmosphere and the sheer sense of wonder of being down there.

Jez's photos do that extremely well, and make the technically challenging task of taking such pictures – saltwater and cameras most definitely don't mix – seem effortless. The ocean is, after all, an alien environment, and whether as snorkellers or scuba divers, we are incredibly lucky to be able to explore it with relative ease.

Thailand is blessed with some of the best reefs and most spectacular marine life in the world, which are both accessible and affordable – a rare combination. As such, for many people, whatever their nationality, Thailand is where they first truly fall in love with the ocean. I know that's what happened to me. And that sense of wonder about Thailand's underwater world – the wow moment – is what I wanted to capture in this book.

This is by no means a comprehensive marine-biology identification manual of the thousands of fish and coral species in Thailand's waters, or a blow-by-blow guide to dive and snorkel sites. *Thailand's Underwater World* is instead a celebration, a Greatest Hits, of the marine life that has continually amazed both Jez and me over 20 collective years of diving in Thailand. It's an attempt to convey something of what we've seen underwater and bring it back for others to enjoy and marvel at, whether or not they have any intention of getting in the water themselves.

One of the best things about scuba diving in Thailand is that you get to meet a lot of great people along the way. Sharing the excitement of discovering the underwater world with others is part of what makes it so special – and the friendships formed in so doing are long-lasting.

My thanks to Jez, Greg Lowe, Mark Soo and Justin Lau for creating the book with me; to dive guides Rob Lee on Koh Lanta, Clive White in Khao Lak, and Ayesha Cantrell on Koh Tao, who've continually shared their special discoveries in Thailand's seas with me and put up with some pretty silly questions too; live-aboard owners Joe and Nute Hue, who gave me a lot of help and encouragement when I was first starting out in Thailand; and all my dive buddies past and present. Most of all, thanks to my mum and dad, who first showed me the sea, and tactfully avoided any subsequent discussion about ever getting a real job.

Preface

Jez Tryner

"

MY APPROACH TO TAKING UNDERWATER PHOTOS HAS ALWAYS BEEN TO TRY AND CAPTURE THE ANIMAL AND SOME OF THE CHARACTER OR ATMOSPHERE OF THE MOMENT.

"

Chris is the literary one of the two of us, as will soon become apparent, and also the driving force and dynamo for making this book happen. It has been a long time in coming, and has had numerous incarnations along the way with many a debate about "the direction we were going", and in the end, after a few beers at sunset on various boats in various tropical locales, it was clear the best plan of attack was to leave it to Chris and hope the words match the pictures.

My approach to taking underwater photos has always been to try and capture the animal and some of the character or atmosphere of the moment. Working in a dense medium that is constantly moving you and your camera and trying to shoot creatures that don't want to be shot means that underwater photography is never boring and constantly challenging.

Having always been of a similar mind to Chris about the wonders of Thailand's underwater world, I am very happy to see it in print and hope that you can pick up on, in some small way, the love Chris and I have for the ocean and its myriad creatures.

Thanks to Greg Lowe and Mark Soo for putting up with my stupid questions and total lack of knowledge about what it takes to make a book, and their unending patience and emails.

Much love and thanks goes out to my parents, who after only ten years stopped asking when I was going to come home and get a real job; hopefully their black sheep has now repaid some of their patience and understanding.

Most of all I would like to thank Chris for putting up with my artistic temperament, and being a lover of fine beer and all things hedonistic, which made this meeting of minds possible.

I hope you enjoy the book.

THAILAND DIVE AREA MAP

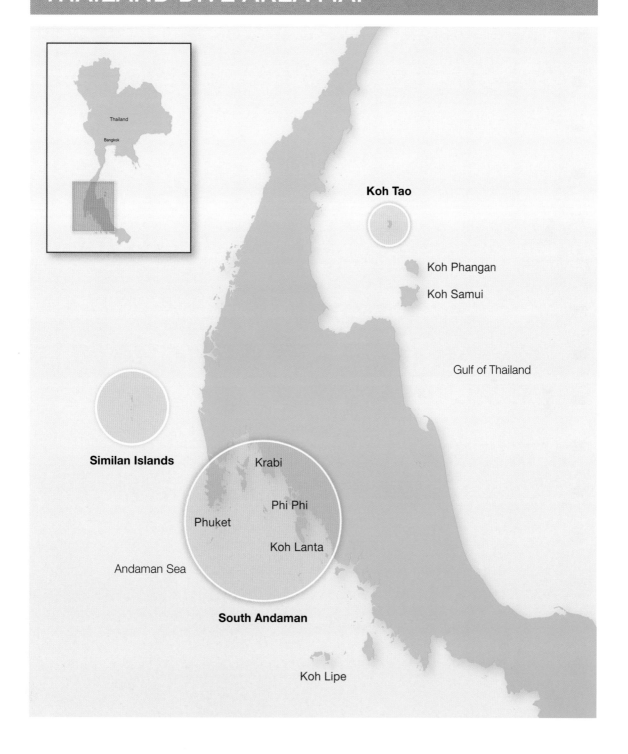

Introduction

With over 3,000 kilometres of coastline facing two oceans, Thailand is as much defined by the water that surrounds it as by the land itself. As the most popular country for tourists to visit in South East Asia, Thailand is legendary for the beauty of its beaches and the friendliness its people. And because the sea is warm, calm, and usually crystal clear, it's also where many people first start to really explore the ocean.

Entering the ocean means entering another world. There's an astounding variety of marine life in Thailand's waters, with over 4,000 species ranging from the majestic but harmless whale shark, which grows up to 12 metres long, to the tiny but explosively colourful nudibranchs that hide among the reef corals. It's a sensory overload of new sights and discoveries, and for many the beginning of a continuing fascination with the sea. *Thailand's Underwater World* provides an insight into this incredible environment, highlighting some of the most spectacular creatures and corals that can be seen in Thai waters.

There are three main areas for diving and snorkelling in Thailand: the Similan Islands on the west coast; the South Andaman, which takes in the area east of Phuket and west of Krabi; and Koh Tao, in the Gulf of Thailand, on the east coast of the country. The west coast faces into the Andaman Sea, part of the Indian Ocean, while the Gulf is part of the South China Sea, which itself belongs to the Pacific Ocean. There are several other notable spots to dive in Thailand, like the shipwrecks in Pattaya and the reefs of Koh Chang, but to have the best chances of seeing coral reefs at their finest and encountering otherwise elusive marine creatures, these are the three key areas.

Thailand's oceans are dynamic and ever-changing, and occasionally, dangerously mercurial too. Animals move around, disappear for months at a time, and then sometimes inexplicably return; as such, the general vicinity they are most likely to be seen in has usually been highlighted rather than a specific locale. It's the ocean, after all, not an aquarium. Going into the ocean with a set agenda about what to see usually leads to disappointment; much better to enter with an open mind and see what surprises await.

Besides being an introduction to the country's marine life, *Thailand's Underwater World* is a visual record of encounters with its ocean inhabitants over the first decade of the 21st century. It's a snapshot of the vibrancy of Thai marine life in those ten years. The threats to this environment, both global and local, are well-known, and their implications are discussed in the final chapter of this book. It's only by continuing to raise the profile of Thailand's underwater world and showing the existence of the unique, irreplaceable creatures within it, that future generations will have any hope of seeing it for themselves.

SHARKS

Menace or Misunderstood?

Sharks
Menace or Misunderstood?

Imagine being in the water with a shark six times your size and weighing nearly 15 tonnes, with a mouth that, at full gape, can open to over a metre in width. It's not the stuff of nightmares, but an experience many snorkellers and scuba divers who come to Thailand dream about: an encounter with the enormous, elusive, and perfectly harmless whale shark.

WORLD'S BIGGEST FISH
The whale shark is officially the biggest fish in the world – growing up to a staggering 12m in length. In keeping with their huge bulk, whale sharks cruise serenely through the water; but while they look as if they move slowly, it takes a champion swimmer to keep up with a whale shark's implacable progress for more than a few minutes.

To be in the water with one of these behemoths is a truly humbling and exhilarating experience, especially as, despite their size, whale sharks remain one of the ocean's most rarely encountered creatures. Little is known about their migratory patterns, their mating habits, or even their numbers – while the whale shark is a protected species in Thailand, they are considered endangered by both CITES (Convention on International Trade in Endangered Species) and the International Union for the Conservation of Nature, and they are hunted across Asia for their fins along with other shark species.

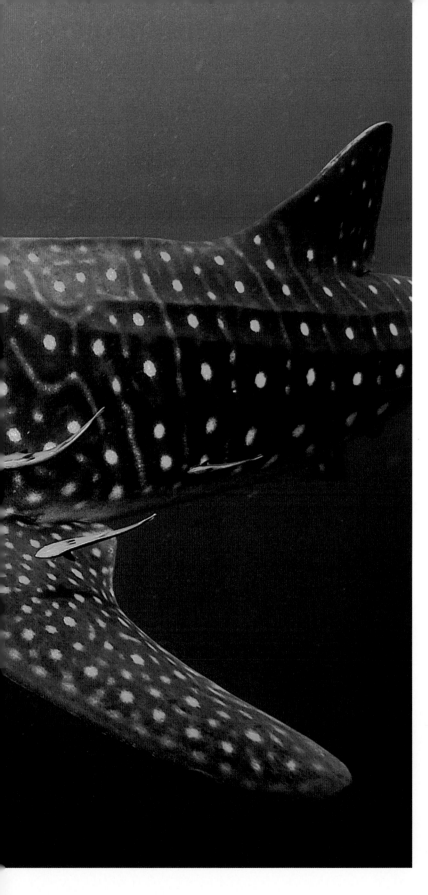

Left: The whale shark dwarfs divers, but is completely harmless to humans.
Previous page left: The whale shark is so big it literally blocks out the sun when it passes overhead.
Previous page right: The whale shark is often trailed by smaller fish who clean their giant brother.

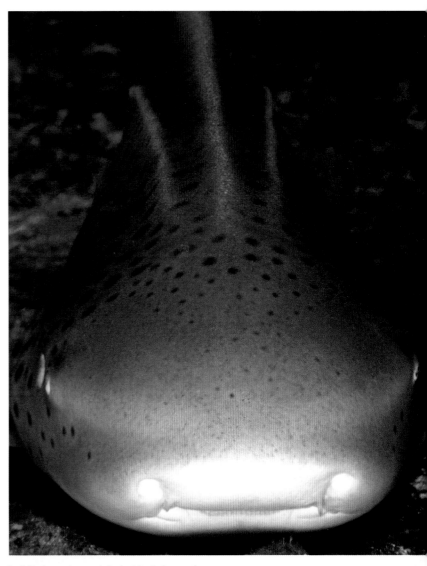

Left & above: Leopard sharks take their name from their distinctive yellow skin and black spots. Relatives of the whale shark, they generally laze on the sand during the day like aquatic cats before hunting at night.

Right: The exquisite eye of the leopard shark.

Photo by Ayesha Cantrell

Above: Grey reef sharks are still occasionally encountered by divers at Koh Tao's Chumphon Pinnacle, where they patrol in packs.

UNDESERVED REPUTATION

Shark populations the world over have been decimated, particularly in Asia, as the demand for shark's fin (the main component of shark's fin soup) has soared with the continent's new prosperity. Sharks are still considered mindless killing machines by many – a view reinforced in the popular imagination by Steven Spielberg's 1975 blockbuster movie *Jaws* – and so their plight gets little sympathy, even though there have been very few shark attacks on humans ever recorded. In Thailand, there are no records of any shark attacks on humans at all. (Great white sharks, incidentally, are not found in Thai waters – they prefer colder oceans like the southern coast of Australia.)

The main species endemic to Thai waters, like grey reef sharks, whitetip and blacktip sharks, are seen less

> " SEEING A SHARK FOR THE FIRST TIME IN THE OCEAN CAN CAUSE A FRISSON OF FEAR, BUT SNORKELLERS AND DIVERS QUICKLY COME TO REALISE THAT THEY POSE NO HARM IF TREATED WITH RESPECT. "

and less now. Even the once-common leopard shark, related to the whale shark, which is relatively easy to locate because it prefers to rest on the sandy bottom napping cat-like during the day, has become harder to find. The leopard shark is one of the most distinctive-looking creatures in Thai waters; its yellow skin, leopard-like spots, and long, powerful tail give it an appearance unique among shark species.

RESPECT IS DUE

Grey reef, blacktip and whitetip sharks conform more to the expected idea of what a shark looks like, with their sleek, aerodynamic bodies that glide effortlessly through the strongest currents. While seeing a shark for the first time in the ocean can cause a frisson of excitement or even fear, snorkellers and divers quickly come to realise that not only do they pose no harm if treated with respect, they are one of most beautiful creatures to watch move through the water.

Of all Thailand's sharks, grey reefs have the most fearsome reputation, as there have been a handful of incidents elsewhere in the world where they have attacked humans when provoked, although there have been no fatalities. Grey reefs are still occasionally sighted at Chumphon Pinnacle in the Gulf of Thailand, implacably cruising past divers and sometimes coming to investigate. There is an ongoing debate among shark experts whether there are bull sharks amongst Chumphon's resident grey reef shark population too, as some seem to sport the bull's characteristic blunt nose. Given the thousands of divers who have seen the sharks at Chumphon in the last few decades without a single incident, it's high time for their reputation to get a makeover.

WHALE SHARK HOTSPOTS

For all the bad news about other species of shark, Thailand is fortunate to be one of the few countries in the world to have whale shark hotspots – areas where these normally elusive creatures have been known to continually return on an annual basis, usually around March and April. The ocean pinnacles of Richelieu Rock and Hin Muang in the Andaman Sea and Chumphon in the Gulf are magnets for whale sharks, but it's still not quite clear why they reappear there each year.

The whale shark has been an enigma ever since its first sighting in 1828 off the coast of South Africa. Revelations about them are becoming more frequent thanks to this increased interest, the most recent discovery being that while whale sharks move slowly when at the surface and witnessed by humans, they subsequently dive to 1,000 metres deep in a steep de-

scent in search of food, ricocheting between the sunless depths and the shallows.

THE OCEAN'S BALANCE

As more is learnt about the whale sharks, there is also more cause for concern: a study of the relatively large number of sightings and measurements from the last couple of decades indicates that the average size of the whale shark is shrinking, due to their being hunted and the lack of time to reproduce. It's through initiatives like Thailand's protection of whale sharks within its own coastal waters that greater awareness of the whale sharks' movements, numbers and safety can be promoted – but it's an initiative that needs to be extended to all species of sharks so that they can begin to flourish again and so that the balance of Thailand's oceans can be maintained.

Whale Shark

Where to see them:
Similan Islands, South Andaman, Koh Tao

Scientific name:
Rhincodon typus

Life expectancy:
Uncertain – 100+ years

Strange but true:
Despite being the biggest fish in the world at up to 12 metres long, whale sharks only eat microscopic plankton.

Endangered?
Yes

Edible?
Yes

Left: Seeing a whale shark for the first time is the most treasured memory of most divers and snorkellers.

TROPICAL FISH
Thailand's Multicoloured Wonders

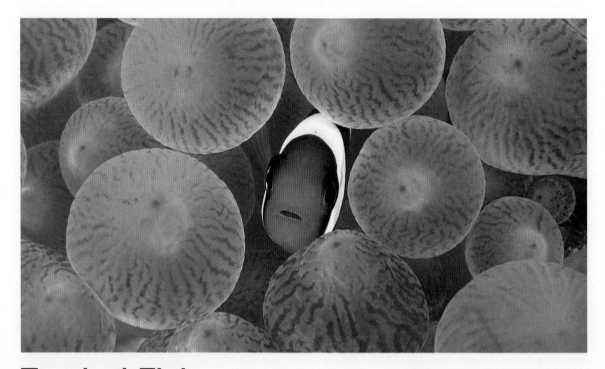

Tropical Fish
Thailand's Multicoloured Wonders

Thailand's coral reefs are a riot of colour beneath the azure sea, and the fish that live on those reefs energise them with a mesmerising dynamism. There are around 4,000 species of fish in Thai waters, making it one of the richest marine coastlines on the planet. The reef itself is a living organism (see page 130–135) and provides a habitat, sustenance and protection for Thailand's exotic fish life.

Among Thailand's thousands of species of fish, some stand out because they school together en masse, and some are noticeable precisely because they are so individualistic and go against the herd mentality.

CUTE AND FEARLESS
Perhaps the most instantly recognisable tropical fish in Thailand – and certainly one of the most sought after – is the clownfish, now eternally famous thanks to Pixar's animated movie, *Finding Nemo*. (Indeed, the Thai name for clownfish is "bpla nemo".) Its unmistakable, bright, white-and-orange stripes, as it peeks out from its host

anemone, are a mesmerising sight for many snorkellers and divers.

The clownfish is just one of numerous species of anemonefish in Thailand, with colours ranging from black with red stripes to bright pink. All of them live in a symbiotic relationship with their host anemone, providing sustenance for the host while receiving protection from the anemone's stinging hydroids, to which the clownfish itself is immune. There can be an entire family of up to four or five clownfish in one anemone, and they will swim up to investigate any visitors.

Despite their cute appearance, clownfish are actually quite aggressive, and have been known to bump against divers' masks in a fearless, if foolhardy, attempt to chase the divers away. It is hard not to be impressed by the courage of a fish that throws itself against an opponent hundreds of times its size.

The clownfish might look resplendent in their orange-and-white outfits, but for sheer outrageousness, the ap-

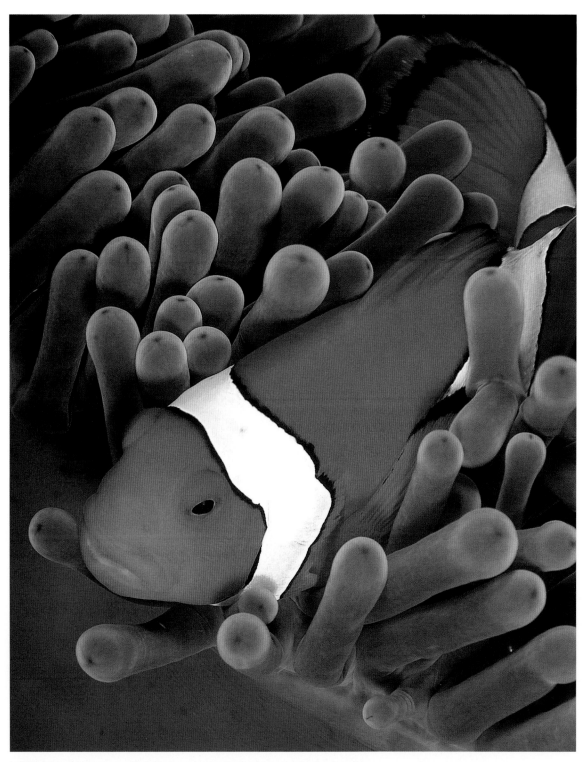

Left & above: Anemones provide both a home and protection from predators for clownfish.

Above: The rarely seen juvenile clown triggerfish is a dazzling mix of colours and patterns.
Right: The adult clown triggerfish looks like an explosion in a paint factory.

Above: The almost-human face of the sweetlips looks permanently worried about something.
Right: The flat, large form of the batfish is often seen hanging around Thailand's reefs.

pearance of the clown triggerfish is hard to beat. It's hard not to laugh when you first see one of these fantastically dressed fish – from the circle of yellow round its mouth to the black mask across its eyes and the glorious circular splotches of white on its underbelly that look like they have been painted on – the clown triggerfish seems designed to entertain.

SWEET LIPS AND SWIMMING DICE

There are many other interesting-looking fish often seen on Thai reefs too. The yellow-and-white striped sweetlips is well-named for its large, almost-human mouth, while the dark red big eyes fish looks perpetually worried.

Another, the parrotfish, owes its permanent grin to its beak, with which it enthusiastically attacks the reef at mealtimes – the sound of it crunching coral can often be heard underwater.

More peculiar still is the tiny pine cone fish, which is very difficult to find as it prefers to hide deep within the base of coral outgrowths, but its unique appearance makes it resemble nothing less than a mobile aquatic pineapple. Also high on the strange-but-cute list is the bright yellow, black-spotted boxfish, known by its scientific name, *Ostra-*

cion cubicus. It really does look like a living, breathing cube. Baby boxfish can sometimes be spotted, and their tiny size makes them deserving of their nickname, "swimming dice". The boxfish is related to the porcupine fish, a fish that swells up like a balloon if threatened. These are found everywhere in the waters of Thailand, as are several species of angelfish, whose beauty tends to be overlooked a little because they are so common. However, the angelfish family does possess a rare member that is the highlight of any dive if discovered – the juvenile emperor angelfish. It is only a few centimetres long but resplendent in swirling vivid blues, blacks and whites. The angelfish's youthful livery will change completely as it grows to maturity and becomes several times larger.

SCHOOL PLAYS

There are fish of all sizes in Thai waters, but one of Thailand's most noticeable fish is also one of its smallest – the glassfish. This is because glassfish tend to school together, sometimes many thousands strong. Their tiny bodies are largely transparent and so reflect the sunlight. When the school moves together in perfect synchronicity, it gives the appearance of a moving ribbon of light over the reef.

Left & above: The juvenile emperor angelfish (left) is one of the smallest but most spectacular fish in Thailand. It completely changes colours as it grows into an adult angelfish (above).

“

THE FISH THAT LIVE ON THAILAND'S CORAL
REEFS ARE WHAT PROVIDE THESE REEFS
WITH A MESMERISING DYNAMISM AND
ENERGY. ”

Above & right: Barracudas are often seen in Thailand,
the small juveniles that school en masse (right) growing
into large solitary hunters that patrol the Thai oceans.

Above: Two bannerfish get up close and confrontational at Elephant Head Rock in the Similan Islands.
Left: Jacks and glassfish congregate around a reef's soft corals.
Next page: One of the few truly aggressive creatures in Thailand's oceans, the meaty triggerfish is not to be messed with when defending its nest.

Several other fish species that provide spectacular displays when they school together include the small and brightly coloured anthias, the archetypal reef fish seen in most video footage of Thailand's reefs, as they rise and fall together in perpetual motion over their home patches of coral. Also present in large numbers are clouds of butterfly fish and banner fish, trailing their distinctive pendants behind them.

It's not just small fish that like to hang out together on Thailand's reefs – their bigger brothers and sisters also congregate together, often putting on breathtaking displays. Batfish are a firm favourite of divers because they are often seen in large schools around mooring lines used for boats, especially in the Gulf of Thailand. They rarely move for anyone or anything. Their large eyes, pursed lips and large, flat, grey bodies tinged with yellow and black make them unique-looking.

Also frequently seen are huge bait balls of yellow snapper in the Similan Islands and South Andaman. Hundreds strong and dominating the reef, they alternately scatter and coalesce in a flurry of yellow and white, glinting in the sunlight, instinctively coordinating their movements to become one.

Big batteries of barracuda regularly appear in Thailand's waters too. Rather than move across the reef, barracuda prefer to hover almost motionless in the blue, looking like a squadron of silver starfighters waiting for orders. Their sleek, long bodies (up to a metre and a half long), elongated mouths and fearsome teeth give them a malevolent air, but their grace as they suddenly stir into action and move rapidly within microseconds of being stationary is breathtaking. Sometimes one can see hundreds of these barracuda, moving in unison in a tightly regimented formation. Breaking through their ranks occasionally are other big fish such as tuna, jacks and trevally – meaty fish that move surprisingly fast for their bulk and show little fear of humans in their territory.

THE MOST AGGRESSIVE FISH

Barracuda have a reputation for being occasionally dangerous, but the scourge of scuba divers, especially around Koh Tao, is the titan triggerfish. While it's related to the comical clown triggerfish, the titan triggerfish is nowhere near as peaceful. It's not venomous, like the lionfish or stonefish or scorpionfish (see Fear Factor, page 164), but the titan triggerfish is, without question, the most aggressive fish in Thai waters.

Building nests in the sand to harbour its young, the titan triggerfish will vigorously defend them against any intruders, including divers. Its relatively large bulk and speed mean it's not a fish to be messed with. The triggerfish regards its territory as an upwards cone, so ascending provides no escape – it will continue to pursue. (Note as well that ascending rapidly whilst diving is incredibly dangerous and should always be avoided). Divers need to turn on their backs, present their fins to the triggerfish – which it might bite – and slowly swim laterally away from the trigger nest.

Tropical Fish: The Anthia

Where to See them:
Similan Islands, South Andaman, Koh Tao

Scientific name:
Anthiinae comes from the Ancient Greek and Swedish for "flower" or "blossom"; named by the grandfather of botany, Carl Linneaus, in 1758.

Life expectancy:
5 years

Strange But true:
Anthias are all born female, but if the male of the group is lost, the largest female can turn herself into a male.

Endangered?
No

Edible?
No

Left & above: Two of the funniest fish to be encountered in Thai waters: the irresistible boxfish (sometimes called "the swimming dice") and the pine cone fish, which bizarrely resembles a mobile aquatic pineapple.

Left: The eternally quizzical gaze of the bright red big eye.

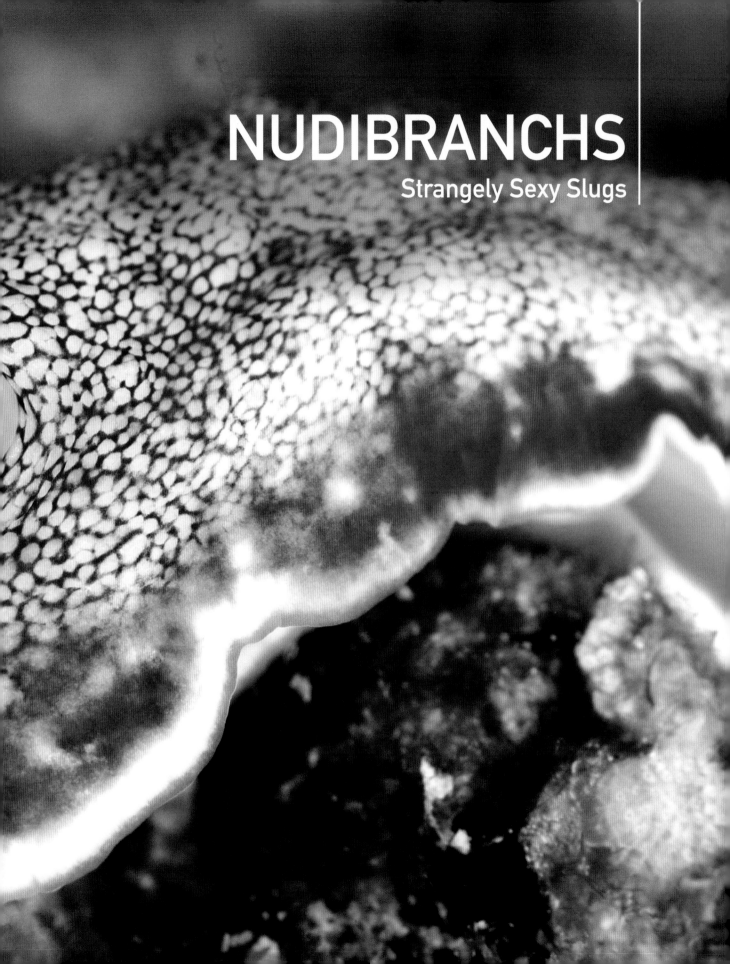

NUDIBRANCHS
Strangely Sexy Slugs

Nudibranchs
Strangely Sexy Slugs

Slugs – not a word you associate with beauty. But for many explorers of Thailand's oceans, the tiny sea slugs known as nudibranchs are a constant source of wonder, with their seemingly infinite variety of stunningly vivid colours and exotic patterns. For a creature that is typically only five or six centimetres long, nudibranchs have a big reputation. Such is the fascination with them that entire encyclopaedias and websites have been devoted to cataloguing more than 3,000 different nudibranch species scattered throughout the Asia-Pacific region, especially as new varieties continue to be discovered each year. The unique colours of nudibranchs have even provided inspiration for fashion designers.

Within Thailand, the dive sites of Koh Haa and Richelieu Rock are particularly good places to search for nudibranchs, and even find a flabellina, a distinctively different nudibranch with rows of delicate, brightly coloured fronds (known as cerata) along its back.

PRETTY BUT POISONOUS

Affectionately referred to as nudis by enthusiasts, nudibranchs may be pretty but some are actually poisonous (although not dangerous to humans, unless eaten). The more vivid its colours, the more toxic a nudibranch's defences. Poisonous nudis get their venom from the sea sponges that they eat, storing the sponge's own poison for their self-defence.

Other species of nudibranch have become impervious to the stinging of hydroids and so can hide within their otherwise dangerous fronds and even eat them

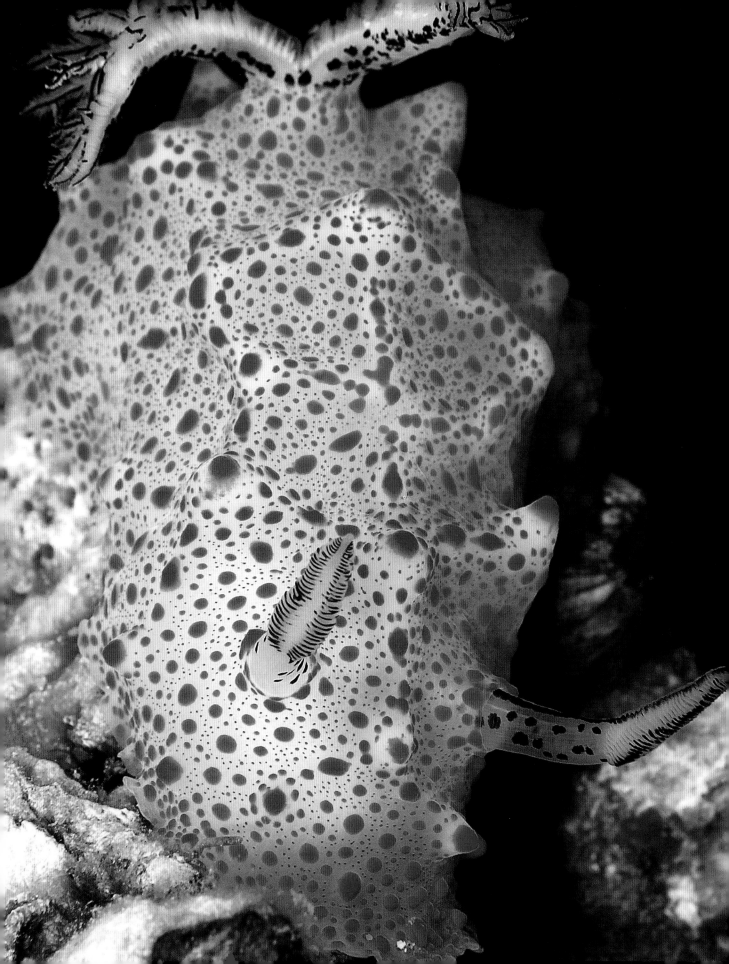

This page: As well as a toxic warning to enemies, the bright colours of a nudibranch let it blend in on the reef. **Previous page left:** With a texture that looks almost like velvet and colours to match, it's no surprise that nudibranchs have inspired fashion designers. **Previous page right:** This warty sea slug has incredibly bright orange pustules on its milk-white body.

Above: This *Aldisa erwinkoehleri* nudibranch mimics the appearance of the common *Phyllidia* sea slug.
Right: With a back that looks like it's carrying fire-tipped spears, the flabellina is one of the most resplendent nudibranchs.

"

THE UNIQUE COLOURS OF NUDIBRANCHS HAVE EVEN PROVIDED INSPIRATION FOR FASHION DESIGNERS.

"

to eat one another if hungry – so those romantic overtures might actually be the precursors to securing a nudi's next meal. If the nudibranchs survive the rigours of mating, they lay a ribbon of eggs, the appearance of which varies enormously between different nudi species, but typically taking the form of a bright yellow coil. These egg ribbons can be almost as beautiful in their shape and colour as the nudis themselves. And so, the nudis continue to create the next generation of pretty but poisonous, affectionate yet cannibalistic sea slugs that will continue to captivate divers in the waters of Thailand.

without harming themselves. In fact, the bright colouration of nudibranchs allows them to match the intense hues of their surroundings and blend in with the coral reefs they inhabit, thus avoiding the detection of predators.

LOVE AND DEATH

Nudibranchs are very friendly with their own kind, often "tailgating" nose to tail as they slowly ooze their way on trails of mucus to maintain physical proximity to one another. This is considered by marine biologists to be a courting behaviour before mating, with one nudibranch showing interest in the other. They are able to find each other initially because of the chemical sensors – or rhinopores – on the top of their heads. Given nudis are hermaphrodites – that is, they have both male and female sex organs – they have the potential to mate whenever they encounter another one of their species.

For such cute creatures, however, nudis have an alarming predilection for cannibalism – they are known

Nudibranchs

Where to see them:
Similan Islands, South Andaman, Koh Tao

Scientific name:
Nudibranchia comes from the Latin *nudus*, naked, and the Greek *brankhia*, gills.

Life expectancy:
From a few days to a few months, depending on species.

Strange but true:
Some species of nudibranchs are able to eat poison from sea sponges and turn it into venom to protect themselves from predators.

Endangered?
No, but reliant on the health of the reef to survive.

Edible?
No.

Left: Nudibranchs deposit egg ribbons from which larvae will hatch out and then eventually progress to baby nudibranchs, some with a lifespan of just a few weeks.

Above: The fantastic yellow and black rabbit nudibranch, technically known as Thecacera.
Left: The tree-like sprouting at the back of this nudibranch are actually branchial plumes that let it breathe.

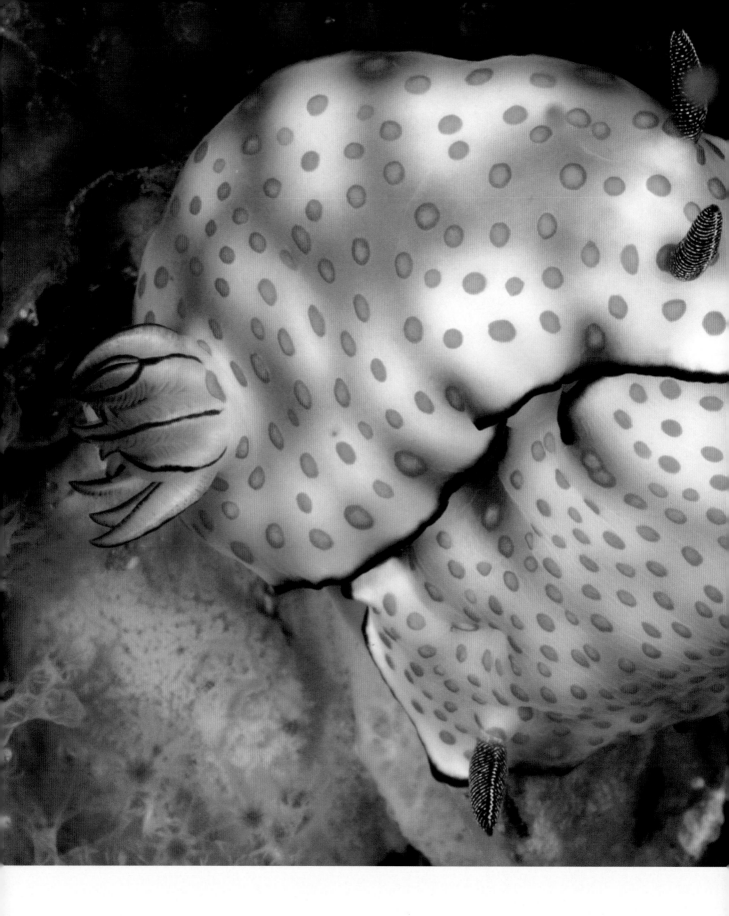

Left: Two nudibranchs mating top to toe.

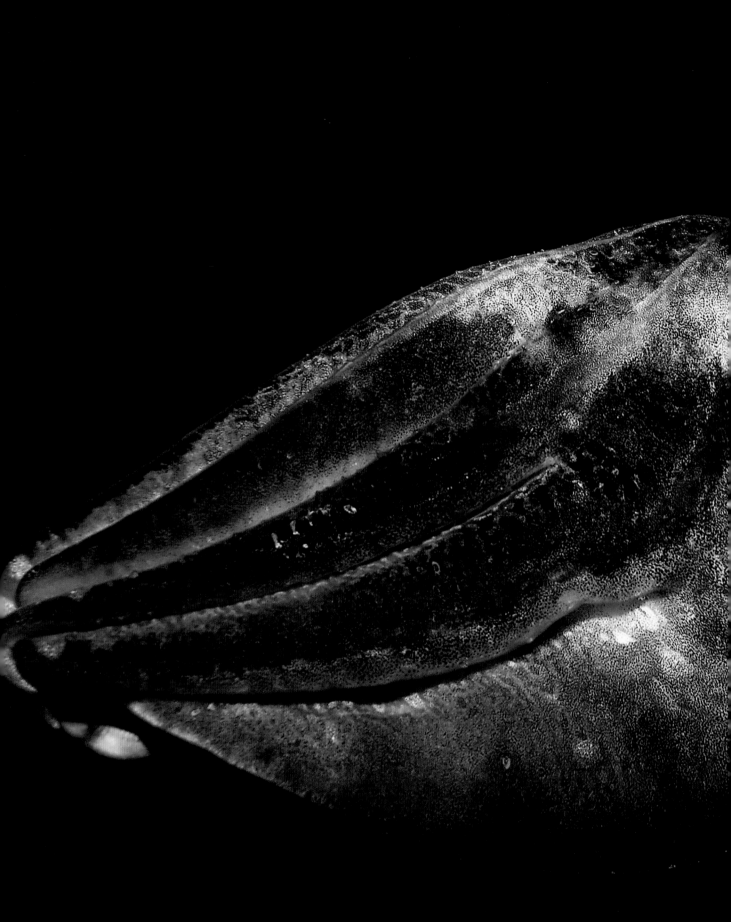

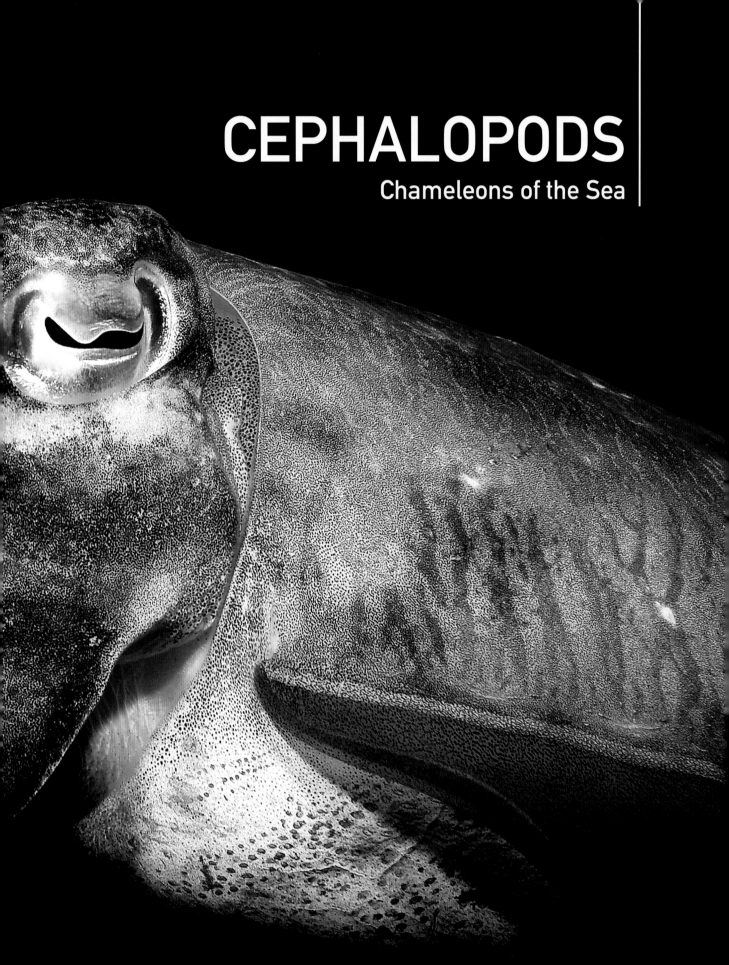

CEPHALOPODS

Chameleons of the Sea

Cephalopods
Chameleons of the Sea

Octopuses, cuttlefish and squids are three of the most fascinating creatures found in Thailand's oceans. Collectively, they are referred to as cephalopods, and share between them the shape-shifting, colour-changing qualities that make them so amazing to behold.

OCTOPUSES
Masters of disguise, octopuses are able to change their colour to blend into the background. Their lack of any internal skeleton means that octopuses can squeeze into the tiniest fissures within coral reefs, pouring themselves in like liquid and disappearing from view within seconds. When spotted, octopuses are usually motion-

less on the reef, either resting or staying stock still to pounce on nearby prey. The craggy pinnacles of Hin Daeng and Hin Muang and the sandy shallows of East of Eden in the Similan Islands provide ideal habitats for octopuses to hide and hunt.

While they are generally wary of divers and snorkellers and will make a swift exit either into the pores of the reef or by high-speed jet propulsion in the opposite direction, octopuses will sometimes actually investigate new arrivals in their domain. Considered the most intelligent of invertebrates, octopuses have a natural, almost cat-like curiosity that leads them to occasionally extend a tentative tentacle towards divers – indeed, there have

Above: A form of jet propulsion allows the cuttlefish to rapidly move backwards from any threat, while its skirt – actually a muscular fin – allows it to steer in any direction.
Left: Without a single bone in their body, octopuses are able to occupy the tiniest spaces between cracks in the reef.

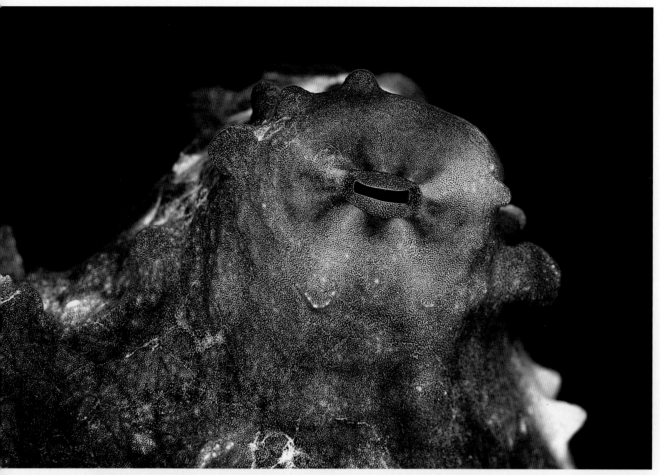

Above: Octopus eyes can always see horizontally from any angle - even if the octopus is upside down. The eye rotates to keep its orientation constant, letting the octopus continually see life on the level.
Right: Like the cuttlefish, the octopus can propel itself through the water rapidly if it wishes, but often prefers to slither across the reef in search of prey.

been incidents where an octopus has playfully snatched a video camera out of a diver's hand and escaped over the reef with it before depositing it a few metres away.

Watching an octopus in motion is an incredible sight, as it streamlines its eight legs behind it and speeds like a rubbery torpedo through the water, propelled by the water that is expelled from its body through a muscular siphon. If an octopus feels particularly threatened, it will also shoot out a cloud of black ink to confuse predators while making its escape. Usually, though, its ability to rapidly change its colour and squeeze itself into the tiniest holes of the reef is enough to keep it safe.

CUTTLEFISH

While Thailand's octopus population have remarkable colour-changing abilities, the real chameleon is the cuttlefish. Not only can they blend into the background like their octopus relatives, they can also put on a spectacular display of pulsating strips of colour if they feel threatened. This is where alternating stripes of colour rapidly pass along its body so that it really does look like a disco is going on inside the cuttlefish. These colour changes not only help the cuttlefish camouflage and defend itself, but also work as a method of communication with other marine creatures.

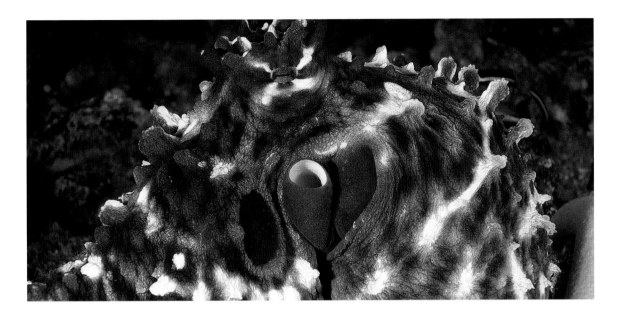

> **OCTOPUSES HAVE A NATURAL, ALMOST CAT-LIKE CURIOSITY THAT LEADS THEM TO OCCASIONALLY EXTEND A TENTATIVE TENTACLE TOWARDS DIVERS.**

Cuttlefish don't squeeze themselves into hidey-holes in the reef as they have a cuttlebone that provides structure for their bodies, and so offer better value for snorkellers and divers in terms of viewing. They are not as skittish as the octopus – they will keep backing slowly away from humans and only fire ink and shoot away like a streamlined missile if provoked by sudden movements.

SQUIDS

Like cuttlefish, squids are one of the staple foods of Thailand, and the lights of fishing boats switched on at dusk on the horizon to attract squids to the surface are a common sight from island beach bars. The shallow waters are also where usually elusive squids are occasionally seen at dusk and dawn as they travel in formation, up from the depths where they have spent the day under the cover of darkness, to spend the night in the warmth near the surface.

Octopus

Where to see them:
Similan Islands, South Andaman

Scientific name:
The octopus belongs to the order Octopoda, which comes from the Greek *oktapous*, eight-footed.

Life expectancy:
A few months to a couple of years, depending on species. Male octopuses die a couple of months after mating.

Strange but true:
Octopus have not one but three hearts.

Endangered?
No, but in danger of being overfished

Edible?
Yes

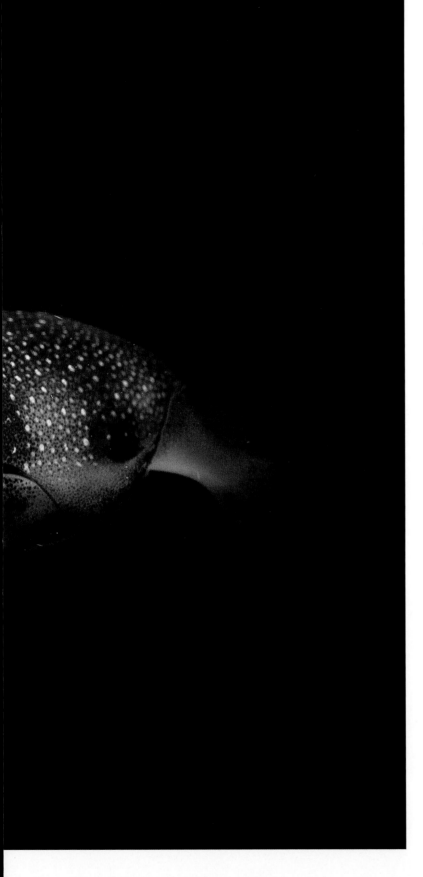

Left: A squid pounces on its fish prey in midwater and quickly drags it into its mouth by using its arms.

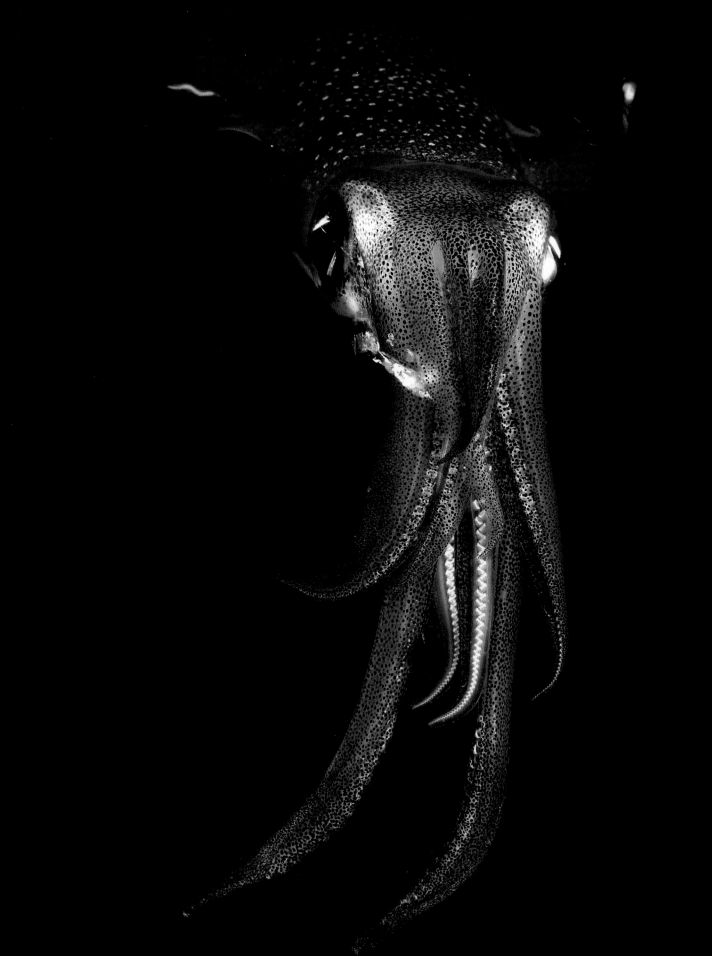

Above: By spreading their tentacles and arms wide, cuttlefish make themselves appear larger to
ward off predators. They also use them to grasp one another during mating as well as to capture prey.
Left: Like the cuttlefish, the squid has eight arms and two tentacles for grappling.

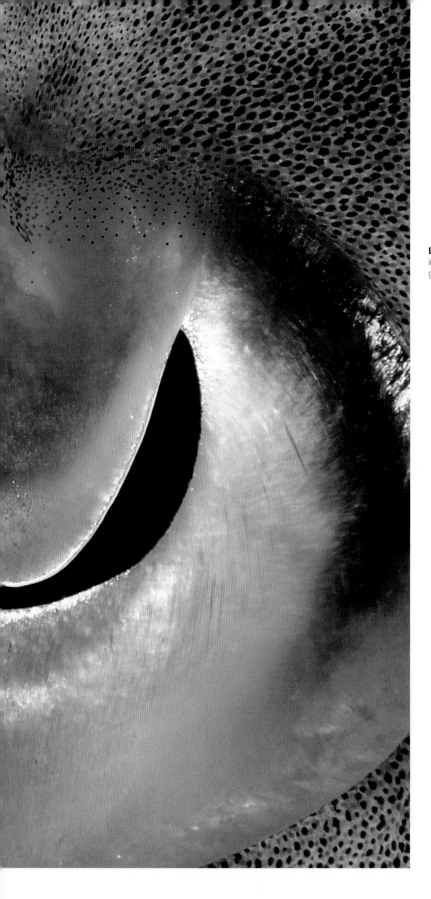

Left: The enigmatic eye of a cuttlefish, the most intelligent of invertebrates. We can only wonder what goes on in their minds.

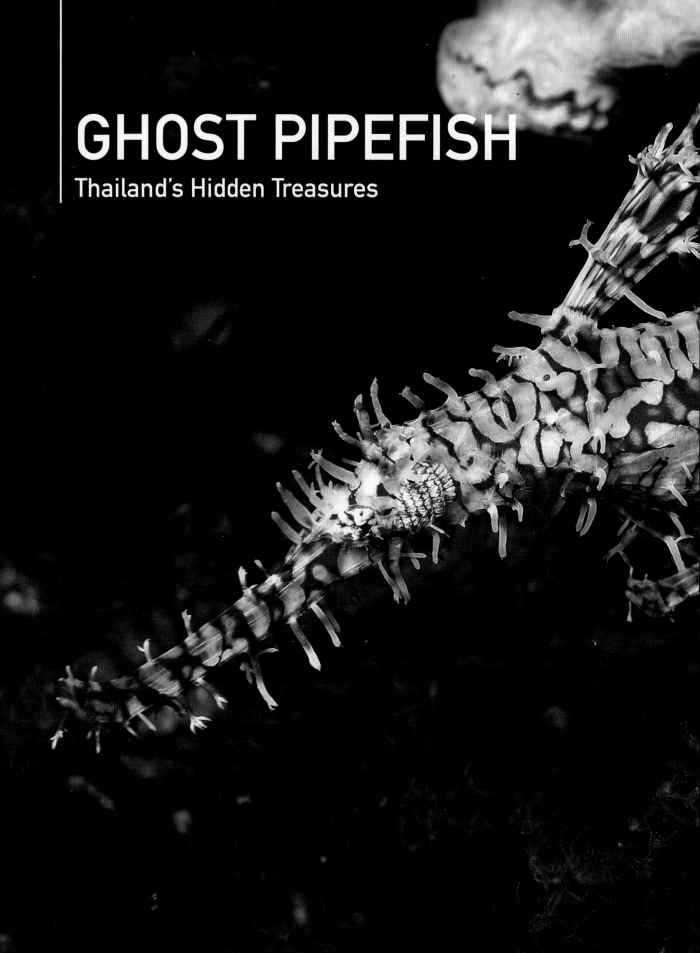

GHOST PIPEFISH

Thailand's Hidden Treasures

Ghost Pipefish
Thailand's Hidden Treasures

Ghost Pipefish – an intriguing name for one of Thailand's most elusive and beautiful marine creatures. The ornate ghost pipefish, or harlequin ghost pipefish, as it's also known, is incredibly difficult to locate because of its small size (it's less than 15cm long) and because it can blend in effortlessly with its environment. Its elongated, elegant snout and luminous, dark eyes are similar to those of the seahorse, to which it's related, but its body is completely different – a fragile, wafer-thin strip fringed with sharp-looking, spiky fronds and small fins. The fins will flare on occasion, to make the ornate ghost pipefish seem bigger, possibly as a threat display. Most striking of all about a ghost pipefish, however, is its colour – from snow white to dark red, from bright yellow to jet black, ghost pipefish have one of the most spectacular liveries of any creature in Thailand's oceans.

BLENDING INTO THE BACKGROUND
Ghost pipefish are so hard to find because they blend in perfectly with crinoids, which are marine animals that

> " MOST STRIKING OF ALL IS THEIR COLOUR — FROM SNOW WHITE TO DARK RED, FROM BRIGHT YELLOW TO JET BLACK, GHOST PIPEFISH HAVE ONE OF THE MOST SPECTACULAR LIVERIES OF ANY CREATURE IN THAILAND'S OCEANS. "

look like fringing plants on the coral reef. The most common crinoid is the feather star, the colour of whose fronds the ghost pipefish are so effectively able to mimic that they seem to disappear. The ghost pipefish usually hang motionless and vertical in the water, so as to follow the lines of the crinoid's fronds and they use their snouts to suck in any unsuspecting tiny crustaceans that pass by.

The best way to look for them is to carefully examine every crinoid on the reef – a treasure hunt which can often prove fruitless. Richelieu Rock, Koh Haa and the bommies at East Of Eden are three of Thailand's

Left & above: Few other creatures above or below water have the delicate beauty of the ornate ghost pipefish. Only a few centimetres long, these tiny creatures are intricately patterned, even around their eyes.

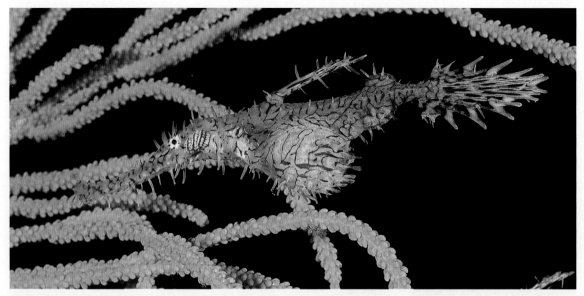

Above: The ghost pipefish's stunning colours are not merely decorative – they provide an artful camouflage that makes the ghost pipefish almost impossible to locate within a crinoid
Right: The tiny eyes of baby ghost pipefish waiting to be born are visible within the egg sac carried by their mother.

sprawling dive sites where ghost pipefish have been spotted, but looking for ghost pipefish at each is like trying to find a needle in an aquatic haystack.

When a ghost pipefish is finally located, however, it's the highlight of any dive. If divers are very lucky, they may even encounter a family of three or four ghost pipefish at different stages of development, living beside the same crinoid.

CHANGEABLE LIVERIES

Ghost pipefish don't begin life in a particular colour – baby ghost pipefish set adrift by their mother on the sea currents to fend for themselves (some 300 at a time from a specially incubated pouch) are transparent. As they are so small and delicate, they are swept across the ocean until they end up on a reef and a crinoid.

When a ghost pipefish finds a feather star to call home, it then magically transforms into the colour of its chosen crinoid. If it drifts too far away and cannot return to its crinoid, it will attach itself to another, adopt the new colour and so disappear within the coral reef once again.

Ghost Pipefish

Where to see them:
Similan Islands, South Andaman

Scientific name:
Solenostomus paradoxus

Life expectancy:
2 years

Strange but true:
Ghost pipefish begin life transparent, then change colour to match their chosen crinoid.

Endangered?
No

Edible?
No

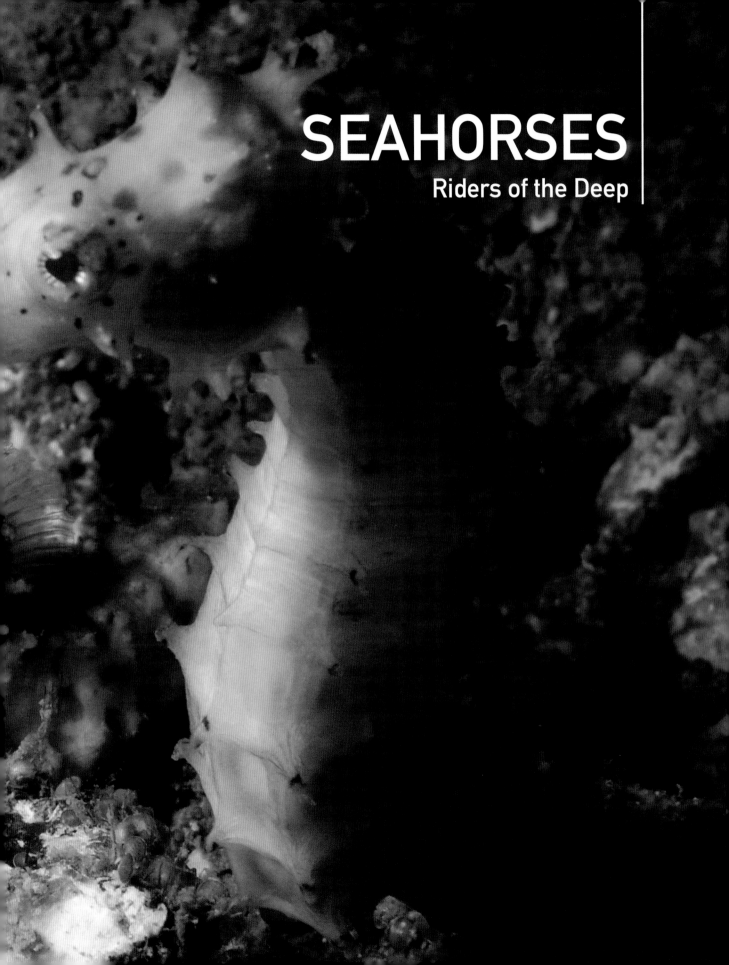

SEAHORSES

Riders of the Deep

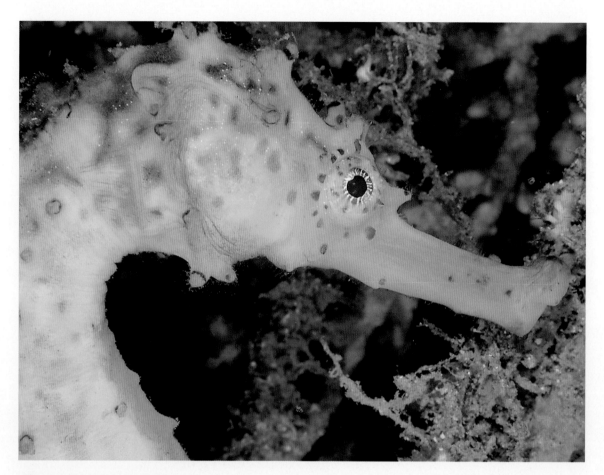

Seahorses
Riders of the Deep

Probably the most instantly recognisable of all of Thailand's marine life, seahorses have long captivated the imagination of those who encounter them. These tiny creatures with their delicate equine faces, large intelligent eyes and elegant S-shaped bodies have fascinated people for thousands of years and become part of ancient legend in several cultures around the world. Ancient Greek and Roman mythologies depict seahorses as fearsome half-horse and half-sea-serpent combinations, and describe them as Poseidon's steed, drawing the chariot of the Greek god of the sea. This is where the seahorse's technical name, *hippocampus*, comes from, derived from the Greek words for "horse" and "sea monster".

SHYEST OF THEM ALL

The name reflects the confusion that 19th-century scientists felt in trying to classify this extraordinary creature. It seems a particularly ironic description given that there are few creatures as non-threatening, beautiful and placid as a seahorse. Indeed, if most of Thailand's marine life is rightfully quite wary of human contact, seahorses are the shyest of all. They tend to hide in the cracks and crevices of reefs, anchoring their tails to a particular spot where they stay long-term. Seahorses are able to blend into their environment, especially seagrass or coral, and this makes them all the harder to locate. This is an ability they share with their relatives, the ghost pipefish.

Above: Masters of camouflage, seahorses blend in with their environment.
Left: The seahorse's long, delicate snout is used to hoover up food.
Next page: Male seahorses like to remain anchored in one small area.

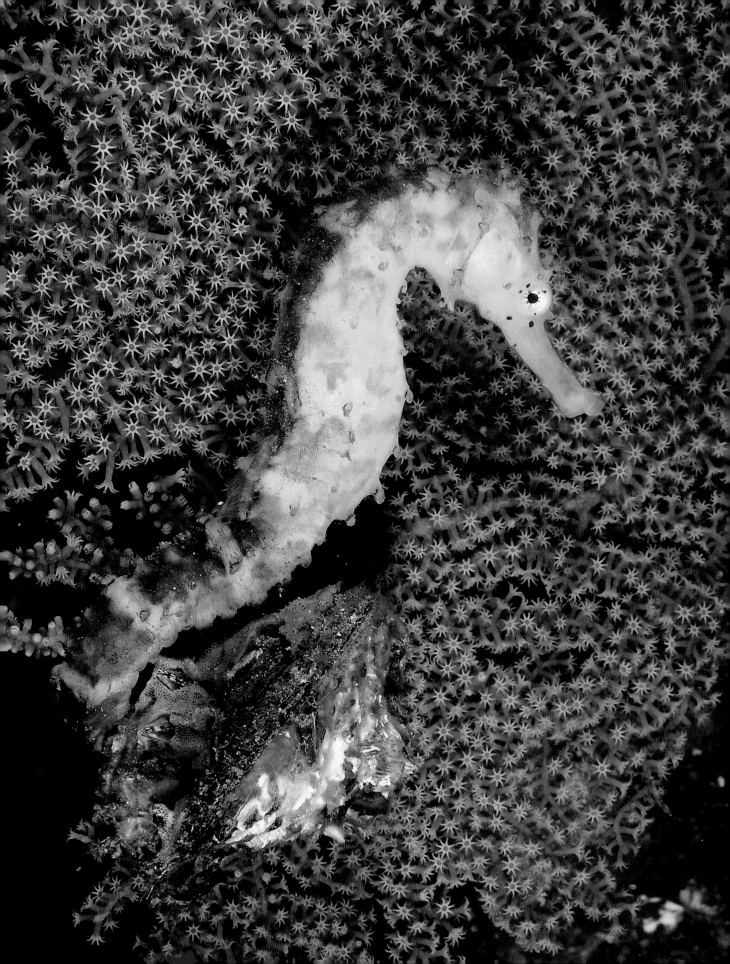

(See page 80; note the remarkable similarity between the seahorse and pipefish snouts.)

Seahorses – unlike ghost pipefish – don't like to drift on currents. They are poor swimmers and not built for moving very far, so they prefer instead to define their territory and stay put. The male seahorse tends to stay within a very small area while the female wanders much further afield before returning to base. Seahorses swim upright, rising and falling with the current; a seahorse in motion is a magical thing to watch.

THESE TINY CREATURES WITH THEIR DELICATE EQUINE FACES, LARGE INTELLIGENT EYES AND ELEGANT S-SHAPED BODIES HAVE FASCINATED PEOPLE FOR THOUSANDS OF YEARS AND BECOME PART OF ANCIENT LEGEND. **"**

FINDING THE SEAHORSE

Seahorses are found throughout Thailand's reefs. They don't mind deep water and have been discovered at nearly 40 metres down at Richelieu Rock – the depth limit for recreational scuba divers.

The tigertail seahorse is perhaps the most commonly spotted seahorse in Thai waters because of its brash colours – a bright yellow livery that's sometimes striped with black, hence the name.

The difficulty in finding seahorses is due partly to their natural wallflower personality, but also partly to the fact that many seahorses have been removed from Thai waters in the last couple of decades. Seahorses form an important part of Chinese medicine, and the rising demand for seahorse parts as ingredients in various potions and remedies makes them an endangered species. It's not uncommon to see bags of hundreds of dried seahorses in Asian markets.

SEX LIFE

With their population threatened, seahorses' mating habits have come under particular scrutiny. They are usually found in pairs and, until recently, were thought to be faithful to one partner for life. But this monogamy has been proven to be largely a myth for most species of seahorse. Researchers have instead established that most seahorses are not only flirtatious, but that around a third of them are fond of same-sex relationships too.

What isn't in question, though, is the seahorse's remarkable role-reversal when it comes to bringing baby seahorses into the world. It's the male seahorse that carries the eggs in its pouch after the mother places them there. There can be up to 2,000 eggs in a pouch, causing it to balloon to a size greater than the width of the seahorse itself. The male seahorse then incubates and fertilises the eggs and eventually releases the babies, setting free hundreds of miniature, fully-formed seahorses into the ocean as the cycle of life begins again.

Seahorses

Where to see them:
Similan Islands, South Andaman, Koh Tao

 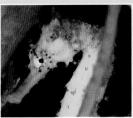

Scientific name:
Hippocampus comes from the Ancient Greek *hippos* for "horse" and *kampos* for "sea monster"

Life expectancy:
Uncertain – 3 to 5 years

Strange but true:
It is the male rather than the female seahorse who carries baby seahorses before they are born.

Endangered?
Yes

Edible?
Yes

MANTA RAYS
Stealth-Bomber Ballerinas

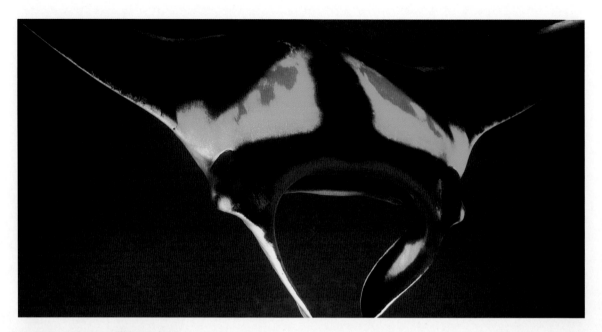

Manta Rays
Stealth-Bomber Ballerinas

It's hard to imagine something as big as a compact car pirouetting on the spot before it launches into a triple spiral twist and an effortless 360-degree backflip – but that's exactly what the black bulk of a manta ray can do when it's feeling playful.

PLAYING WITH THEIR FOOD

Known as "devil fish" to sailors in earlier days because of their size (up to 4 metres wide from wingtip to wingtip) and their ominous appearance, manta rays are in fact completely harmless to humans and are now universally adored by snorkellers and divers alike for their serene presence. They feed on microscopic plankton that live just under the ocean's surface and this is why manta rays are often seen flicking the occasional wingtip out of the water and even sometimes breaching the surface completely while executing playful backflips – they're quite literally playing with their food.

Seeing 1500 kg of manta ray leap out of the water and somersault in the air before splashing back in gives some idea of the incredible dexterity of these creatures. No matter how many videos and photos of manta rays one has seen before, to encounter a manta face to face in real life for the first time is a stunning, euphoric experience, thanks to the impossible grace of their movement in the water.

The largest of all the rays, mantas have no sting at the end of their tails, unlike the commonly seen and much smaller blue-spotted ribbontail ray, which is found buried in the sand virtually everywhere in Thailand. The blue-spotted ray is very shy and tends to shoot off in a flurry of sand particles whenever it spots humans underwater. It has a barb at the end of its tail that can deliver a painful venomous sting, but it's very unlikely to be used against humans as the blue-spotted ray would rather make a hasty exit at the first hint of human contact.

Manta rays are generally elusive creatures, and comparatively little is known about them as they usually stay far away from human habitats. Recent research indicates that there are actually two species of manta – one that migrates huge distances across oceans, and one that largely stays within the same locale.

Above: With a wingspan reaching up to four metres in width, a manta ray is big enough to block out the sun.
Left: Some mantas have distinctive white markings on their topside.

Above: Every manta has unique markings on its underbelly which let scientists identify individuals.

MANTA HOTSPOTS

Thailand is very fortunate in that it has several hotspots where mantas are frequently, if irregularly, spotted – Hin Daeng and Hin Muang off Koh Lanta, and Koh Bon and Richelieu Rock near the Similan Islands – all of which are ocean pinnacles reachable by several hours' boat ride.

Koh Bon has become the most likely place to encounter a manta ray in Thai waters. Its coastline continues as a vertical wall which drops down to the reef below. The mantas cruise in over the reef and hover at particular spots, which are cleaning stations. Angelfish and wrasse hover around the mantas, cleaning them of parasites, thus getting an easy meal while making the manta happy. Remoras, another kind of cleaning fish, can often be spotted physically attached to the manta's underbelly, hitching a ride to ensure the next meal is always nearby. The mantas also like to follow the line of the wall, gliding effortlessly parallel to it and then wheeling away back out into the blue.

ENCOUNTERS WITH THE MANTA

It's not uncommon for manta rays to come quite close to snorkellers and divers who stay still, as they are inquisitive creatures – and if they're busy feeding, they might only break off from their trajectory at the last moment, to avoid a collision with snorkellers. There is some discussion about whether mantas are attracted to or repelled by the bubbles from scuba gear. Some think that mantas like the feel of the bubbles tickling their underbellies, while others think they drive them away. In close encounters, both snorkellers and divers have reported astonishing moments where a manta ray makes eye contact with people around it – mantas are intelligent animals and this is one of their ways of acknowledging the new arrivals in their realm.

In less enlightened times, divers would sometimes hitch a ride on the back of a manta ray; thankfully, word has gotten out that this harms the manta, not only causing it stress but affecting its health because contact with humans can transmit human bacteria to the manta.

Unfortunately, although it is a protected species in Thailand, there's anecdotal evidence that manta rays

NO MATTER HOW MANY VIDEOS AND PHOTOS OF MANTA RAYS ONE HAS SEEN BEFORE, TO ENCOUNTER A MANTA FACE TO FACE IN REAL LIFE FOR THE FIRST TIME IS A STUNNING, EUPHORIC EXPERIENCE.

are increasingly being hunted for their meat in place of sharks, which are becoming scarcer. Given its sheer size, a manta ray can fetch a good sum of money. Ironically, though, manta meat usually ends up being used as fishmeal. It's a grim and unnecessary end for what many people would consider the most spectacular marine creature to be found in Thailand's waters and one of its most iconic tourist attractions.

Manta Rays

Where to see them:
Similan Islands, South Andaman

Scientific name:
Manta birostris

Life expectancy:
Uncertain – estimated at 20 years

Strange but true:
Despite its size, a manta ray only eats microscopic plankton

Endangered?
Yes

Edible?
Yes

Above: Despite its size, the tail of the manta ray doesn't possess a sting.

Left: A snorkeller looks on from the surface as a manta ray wheels below. Mantas frequently come to the surface to feed, giving snorkellers and divers alike the chance of a close encounter.

Next page: The pure whiteness of a manta ray's underbelly is a dramatic contrast to its black wings.

TURTLES
Thailand's Ocean Icons

Turtles
Thailand's Ocean Icons

Perhaps Thailand's most iconic sea creature, the turtle is an integral part of Thai culture. This captivating creature is found throughout the Gulf of Thailand and along the Andaman coast too. In fact, Koh Tao, one of Thailand's major diving destinations, translates as Turtle Island.

HANGING OUT IN THE SHALLOWS

Because they are reptiles, turtles need to periodically come to the surface to breathe, and this is part of the reason why they spend so much time in the shallows. As such, they are one of the easiest of Thailand's marine creatures to spot – not only can scuba divers regularly encounter turtles gracefully cruising through the blue several metres below, but snorkellers can often see turtles resting on the coral reef in the shallows. In fact, one can even view turtles without getting wet – from a boat at

Donald Duck Bay in the Similan Islands and at Koh Haa near Koh Lanta, where they are frequently seen breaking the surface for air. With some planning and luck, it's also possible to see turtles venturing onto the beach at night to lay their eggs.

Turtles inspire so much interest because they're a mixture of the comical and the determined. Their shape looks like an aerodynamic failure, especially when they drag themselves up the beach, but in their natural habitat, it's amazing how fast turtles can glide through the water. Turtles are curious creatures around humans, and will sometimes play around swimmers, snorkellers and divers. (Do note though that, as with all marine creatures, it's important never to touch them, however tempting it is to do so, as human bacteria can be transferred and ultimately kill them.) A turtle feeds on the reef by ripping

Above: Going up: Turtles need to regularly return to the surface for air.
Left: Turtles are often found in the shallows of coral reefs, making for a memorable encounter.
Next page: Scientists are still baffled by the ability of turtles to unerringly travel hundreds of miles back to their birthplace.

"

TURTLES ARE A BAROMETER OF THE HEALTH OF THAILAND'S OCEANS BECAUSE THEIR ABUNDANCE REFLECTS BOTH THE STATE OF THE SEA AND THE BEACHES.

"

great clumps of coral out with its hard beak. When it feeds, it can be so engrossed in its meal that it will completely ignore any human observers.

DWINDLING NUMBERS

While turtles are still a fairly common sight in Thai waters, their population has dramatically decreased (by up to 95 percent, according to some estimates), most recently because of industrial fishing techniques and the encroachment of development on the beaches where turtles go to lay their eggs. Given that turtles mate and give birth at around 20 years of age, it's sometimes the case that they return home to find their once-empty beach completely taken over.

Scientists are still baffled by the unerring navigational ability in turtles. Female turtles typically return to the same beach where they were born to give birth, often from hundreds of miles away, crossing entire oceans, years or even decades after they were last there. While scientists have not managed to work out exactly why or how turtles do this, current research suggests turtles are somehow able to memorise the unique location of their birthplace in the planet's magnetic grid.

Turtle hatchlings generally have a very low survival rate – only around two in one thousand hatchlings survive to become adults – so the destruction of the turtles' traditional hatching grounds has greatly weighted the odds even more against the survival of future turtle generations.

Of the five turtle species endemic to Thailand, only the green, hawksbill, olive ridley and leatherback turtles are left in any significant numbers; the loggerhead turtle has not been spotted for over a decade.

SURVIVAL IN THE BALANCE

There are several turtle conservation programmes in Thailand which try to redress this problem. Perhaps the most famous is the annual turtle hatchling release on Koh Tao, where hatchlings raised by conservationists to ensure their environment is protected are then released into the ocean, along with a lot of encouragement, from locals and tourists alike.

Turtles are a barometer of the health of Thailand's oceans because their abundance reflects both the state of the sea and the beaches. The tenacity of turtles in returning to their beaches and surviving despite the huge odds against them may allow them to thrive once again in Thailand's oceans.

Green Turtle

Where to see them:
Similan Islands, South Andaman, Koh Tao

Scientific name:
The green turtle's name is *Chelonia mydas* – from the Greek *chelone*, meaning tortoise, and *mydos*, meaning wetness.

Life expectancy:
Over 100 years

Strange but true:
Turtles can unerringly navigate hundreds of miles back to the beach where they were born decades before.

Endangered?
Yes

Edible?
Yes

FROGFISH
The World's Ugliest Fish

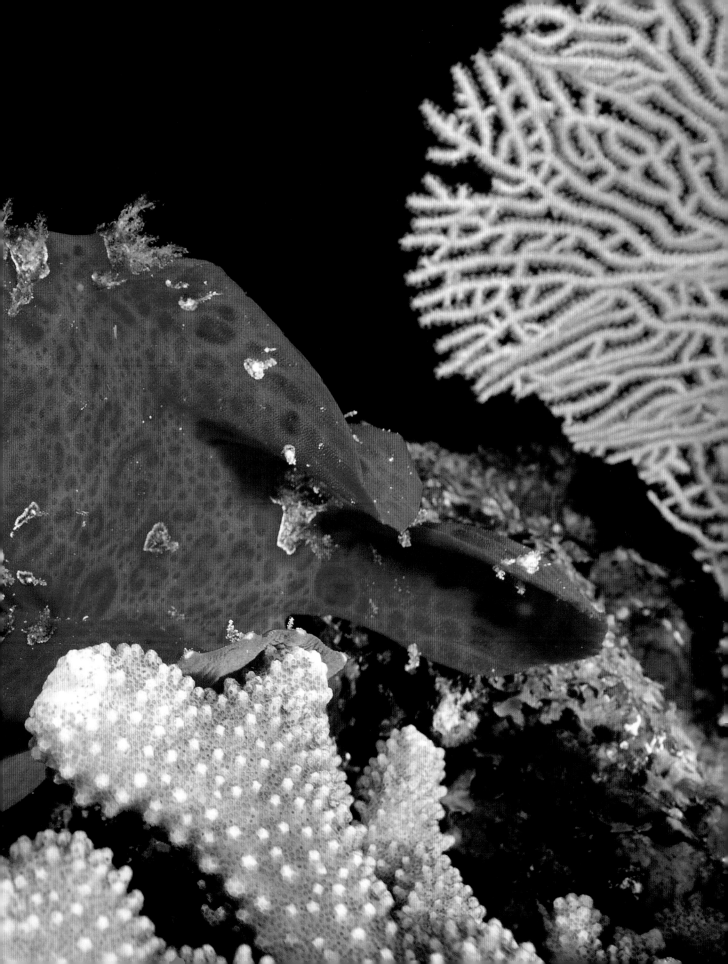

Frogfish
The World's Ugliest Fish

It's a face only a mother could love. The frogfish has the dubious acclaim of being the ugliest fish you'll see in Thai waters – and possibly anywhere in the world. Its lumpen, misshapen face is actually a deeply cunning way for this largely immobile fish to camouflage well with its surroundings, and catch prey by means of the lure hanging enticingly over its barely noticeable mouth. By wiggling the lure to mimic a worm or other small delicacy, the frogfish goes fishing for other fish. Different frogfish species have differently shaped lures – some look like worms or tiny fish, others are shapeless – and the lures can be retracted when they are not required. Frogfish are voracious eaters, happily targeting prey up to twice their size and sometimes eating other frogfish, even potential mates.

SETTLING DOWN AND BLENDING IN
With this highly inventive way of catching prey, there's not much thrill-of-the-chase action with frogfish – they are big fans of finding one spot, usually a crevice between two rocks or at the base of a gorgonian fan, and settling down to wait for each meal to come along. Their patience is rewarded precisely because they become part of the aquatic landscape and are invisible to unwary passersby.

They do not move much but when the frogfish fi-

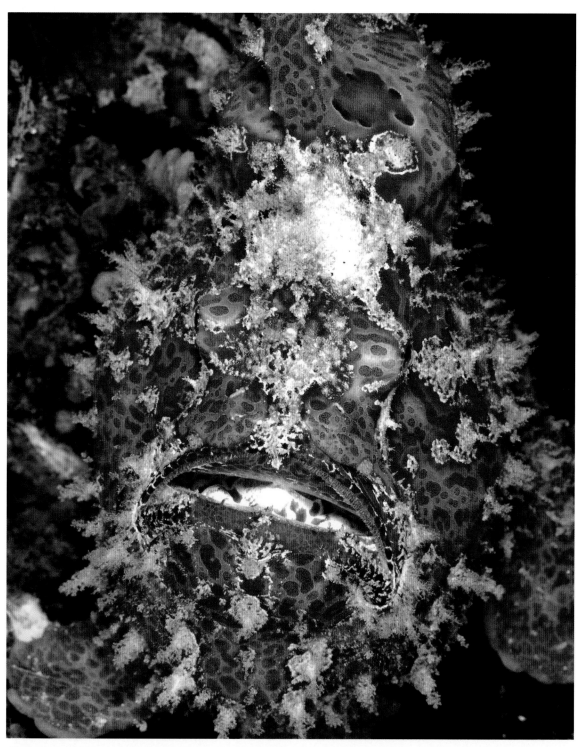

Above: The frogfish's large mouth beneath its lure is almost invisible thanks to its natural camouflage.
Left: Gripping onto the rock with webbed feet like its amphibian namesake, the frogfish patiently waits for its prey.

"
WHILE MANY FROGFISH ARE A DULL GREY COLOUR, IN THAILAND'S WATERS INDIVIDUALS HAVE BEEN FOUND THAT ARE RESPLENDENT IN SHOCKING PINKS, SUN-BRIGHT YELLOWS, FOREST GREENS, AND VELVET BLACK. "

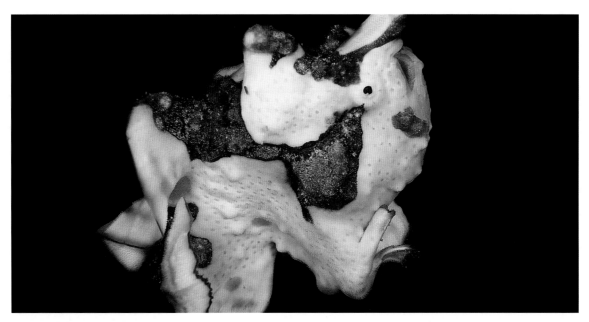

Above & left: The clown frogfish, comparatively smaller and distinctively marked in circus-like vivid reds and yellows, is the nearest this species comes to "cute".

nally decide to go for a swim in search of a new place to perch, they can look quite comical. With only small amphibian-like feet that are great for gripping rocks but are not so good for moving through the water, the frogfish look thoroughly uncomfortable in their moves, making a series of short hops across the sea floor as they propel themselves by expelling water through their gills.

COLOURFUL INDIVIDUALS

While many frogfish are a dull grey colour, the individuals found in Thailand's Similan Islands have been seen resplendent in shocking pinks, sun-bright yellows and forest greens, as well as velvet black. Their colour depends entirely on the surroundings, as frogfish are able to change colour within hours to mimic their new surroundings.

The clown frogfish – so named because of its almost artificially vivid red-and-white livery that looks like circus makeup – borders on cute, especially the baby clown frogfish, which are only a few centimetres long. The whiteness of their faces makes their eyes and mouths a little more apparent and this gives them a permanently quizzical expression.

Frogfish

Where to see them:
Similan Islands

Scientific name:
Antennarius maculates

Life expectancy:
Uncertain – 3 to 5 years

Strange but true:
Frogfish target prey up to twice their size and sometimes eat other frogfish, even potential mates.

Endangered?
No

Edible?
No

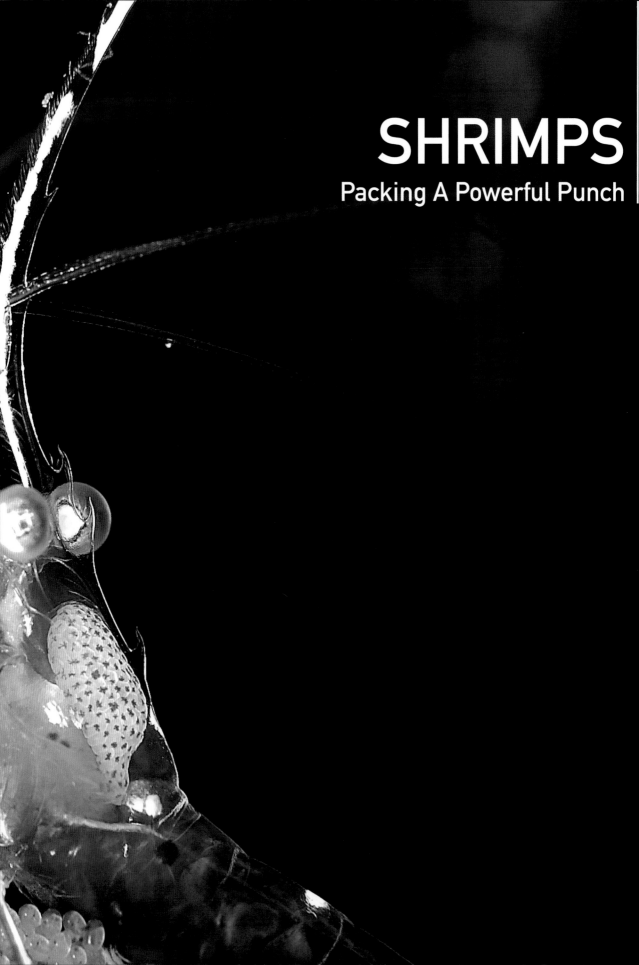

SHRIMPS
Packing A Powerful Punch

Shrimps
Packing A Powerful Punch

The word "shrimp" used to be a popular insult for anyone considered weak – but some shrimps that are found in Thai waters are anything but.

MANTIS SHRIMPS

The peacock mantis shrimp is the Muhammad Ali of Thailand's reefs – it uses a club from within its body to penetrate the shells of its snail prey. Solitary and aggressive, the mantis shrimp is one of the few animals that actively goes out and hunts its prey rather than wait for it to come near its home. So named because of its resemblance to the praying mantis, it uses its two raptorial forelegs to hold on to its prey. Technically, the mantis

shrimp is not a shrimp, but a marine crustacean of the Stomatopod family.

Scientists have been fascinated with the mantis shrimp's devastating delivery mechanism ever since it was found to be able to break aquarium glass when held in captivity – it's that powerful. Because of the mantis shrimp's extremely colourful plumage, it is a very popular choice for aquariums – although it has also been nicknamed the "thumb-splitter" for inflicting wounds on unwary aquarium handlers. Thankfully, mantis shrimps grow to only around 15 cm long so they can't bully every other creature on the reef.

Similar to the peacock mantis shrimps are the spear-

Above: Cleaner shrimp will look after any fish big or small, including the tiny glassfish.
Left: The peacock mantis shrimp harbours the most powerful punch in the animal kingdom, both above and below water.

THE MANTIS SHRIMP IS THE
MUHAMMAD ALI OF THAILAND'S REEFS. ”

Above: The mesmerising eyes of the peacock mantis shrimp revolve in different directions at the same time.
Left: Like a Chinese dragon, the peacock mantis shrimp in full regalia when it emerges from its lair is a sight to behold.

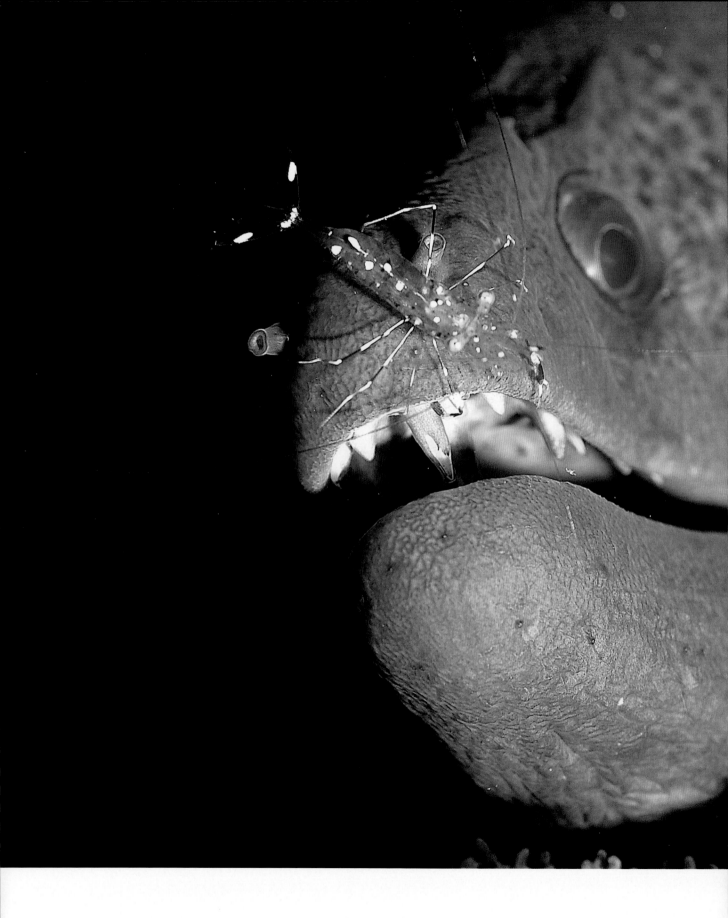

Left: Staring death in the face, the cleaner shrimp confidently cleans in and around the moray eel's mouth without fear of becoming its next meal, thanks to the valuable service it provides.

ing mantis shrimps, but these prefer to remain in one place. Burrowed in holes, they spear their prey passing overhead, again at lightning speed. The eyes of the mantis shrimp – regardless of the variety – are spectacular to look at. Both are oversized and move independently of each other at remarkable angles, so that the mantis shrimp can be looking at you with one eye and 70 degrees to the left with the other.

HARLEQUIN SHRIMPS
Harlequin shrimps are much smaller than mantis shrimps – they are only a few centimetres long. Like the mantis shrimps, they also have remarkable colours, their white-and-orange livery and big paddle-like legs making them quite unique. Usually very difficult to find as they prefer to hide deep in crevices, harlequin shrimps turn suddenly fearless when looking for their next meal. They feed solely on starfish, which are often up to 10 times their own size. Despite the harlequin shrimps' cute appearance, they have the disconcerting habit of paralyzing and dragging the starfish back to their lair and feeding on their victim while they're still alive. They also perform a remarkable if rarely seen ritual prior to mating (see page 136).

CLEANER SHRIMPS
Cleaner shrimps are just as feisty as harlequin shrimps. They are often found in groups on Thai reefs, living in symbiotic relationships with other marine creatures. A common example of this mutually beneficial arrangement is where a cleaner shrimp can be seen doing a seemingly death-defying dance in and around the fearsome jaws of a moray eel, perching on the end of the moray's nose and venturing inside its mouth.

How does their relationship work? The moray could take a human hand off if it looked like lunch, and swallow the cleaner shrimp in one gulp if it wished, but it avoids harming the shrimp because the shrimp does a good job of removing the parasites inside its mouth and those that get attached to the moray's body. For the shrimp, it gets an easy, steady diet and protection too, as predators are likely to be deterred by the moray's presence.

Mantis Shrimps

Where to see them:
Similan Islands, South Andaman, Koh Tao

 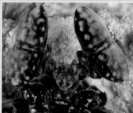

Scientific name:
The peacock mantis shrimp is *Odontodactylus scyllarus*.

Life expectancy:
3 years

Strange but true:
Peacock mantis shrimp can punch so hard they shatter aquarium glass.

Endangered?
No

Edible?
Yes

Left: Few other underwater creatures have as remarkable plumage as harlequin shrimp. They are usually seen together in pairs.
Above & next page: Despite their almost comical appearance, harlequin shrimp are fond of eating starfish alive, one leg at a time.

Above & right: Lurking within its hole waiting for prey to pass overhead, the spearing mantis shrimp uses its incredible optics which can swivel independently of each other to keep watch.

CORAL REEFS

One of Nature's Greatest Creations

Coral Reefs
One of Nature's Greatest Creations

While Thailand's reefs are often referred to as "coral gardens" and "the rainforests of the sea", coral reefs aren't actually plants but animals. The beautiful reefs that cover much of Thailand's coastline are made up of millions of tiny animals called polyps, each a few millimetres long and resembling a sea anemone under a microscope. These polyps grow together in colonies to form the vast collection of hard and soft corals which provide a home and habitat for the thousands of marine animals, big and small, to be found in Thai waters.

Coral reefs are considered one of nature's most incredible and diverse creations, and Thailand has numerous spectacular examples of coral growth that have taken decades, sometimes centuries, for the ocean to create. The Similan Islands, in particular, have a profusion of hard and soft corals that live together in chaotic co-habitation, especially at sites like East of Eden, Anita's Reef and Richelieu Rock. Here, there are large coral bommies – short for *bombora*, the aboriginal word that signifies a clump of coral isolated from the rest of the reef. These coral-covered bommies are suffused with large clouds of glassfish and other creatures. They are probably the most individually stunning parts of Thailand's reefs – East of Eden in particular has been visited by virtually every major television documentary team in the last couple of decades.

Above: Soft and hard corals form an aquatic skyscraper amongst which anemones and their resident clownfish can flourish.
Left: The spectacular colours of Thailand's soft corals rival the brightest neon colours.

Above: Sunlight feeds all the marine creatures that create Thailand's coral reefs, including these stunning soft corals at Hin Daeng.
Previous page: A riot of colour – a deep bommie at East of Eden in the Similan Islands resembles a living, breathing Jackson Pollock painting, suffused with explosively coloured soft corals and surrounded by thousands of glassfish.

HARD CORALS

Hard corals make up the main part of the reef. As the tiny polyps grow, they create a hard calcium carbonate skeleton around them for protection. When the polyp dies, the skeleton remains, and is built on by other polyps. In this way, the size of a hard coral continues to expand year upon year, with the living polyps building on the back of the old skeletons. Over the course of a year, a coral will increase in size by just a few centimetres – the largest corals on the reef are also the oldest, and can date back hundreds of years.

In Thailand, there are numerous types of hard coral that one can see while snorkelling or diving, and whose common names describe their appearance well. Table corals, which can grow to enormous sizes of several metres across, are coral that, from an initial root that anchors them to the reef, pile on top of one other to form a solid plate of coral. They are often found in the shallows where their large surface area can receive maximum sunlight. They can also be seen perched precariously on top of rocky outcrops as the polyps build towards the sun. At the same time, they are fragile and some have been found snapped off at the stem by strong currents or poor fishing practices.

Just as aptly named are brain corals – which have an eerie resemblance to the shape of the human brain – and staghorn corals, which look like the antlers of a deer. The staghorn are particularly hardy and tend to be one of the first corals to grow back in damaged areas.

SOFT CORALS

Soft corals, unlike their hard counterparts, do not leave behind a skeleton as their polyps propagate. Their appearance is similar to thick sprigs of white topped with multiple cauliflower-like heads, set ablaze with extremely bright purples, reds and oranges. En masse, soft corals appear like a technicolor forest, gently swaying in the current, as, for example, at the dive sites of Hin Daeng or Koh Haa in the South Andaman.

Gorgonian fans are one of the most recognisable of soft corals on Thailand's reefs, often growing to sizes larger than a human being. One cannot miss them because the fans, growing out from coral walls or sometimes directly on top of them, have vivid orange, red or pink colours. Their size belies their delicate makeup of hundreds of strands of calcium, which are easily damaged by the slightest contact.

THAILAND HAS NUMEROUS SPECTACULAR EXAMPLES OF CORAL GROWTH THAT HAVE TAKEN DECADES FOR THE OCEAN TO CREATE.

CORALS KEEP US ALIVE

Coral reefs are similar to trees in that their size indicates their age. Like trees, the reefs are also crucial to humans because they play an important part in regulating the world's oxygen supply. Estimates vary, but coral reefs produce around half of the world's oxygen and absorb 30 percent of the carbon dioxide that humans create. Current scientific research has brought up a major concern: the reefs have absorbed as much carbon dioxide as they can. This means that poisonous gases created by human industry will now remain in the atmosphere instead of being removed by the reefs. At the same time, global warming and the rise of sea temperatures are causing ongoing coral bleaching. One of our major ways of disposing of carbon dioxide is reaching capacity, and at the same time is being continually damaged by the effects of climate change.

Besides these alarming global threats, Thailand faces several local problems – its reefs are suffering from pollution, over-development of beach areas, over-fishing and dynamite bombing. As a result, decades-old reefs are being destroyed, sometimes in mere seconds. Although there are protected Thai marine parks, tourism has added to the problems, with too many people allowed into reef areas and subsequently causing damage when they touch or stand on the coral. Calls for greater care of Thailand's reefs are not new. For the last couple of decades, scientists and passionate laypeople have warned that the reefs are being irreparably damaged. The difference is that we now appear to be heading towards a tipping point, and what happens in the next couple of decades could determine whether the reefs survive beyond the end of the 21st century.

Coral Reefs

Where to see them:
Similan Islands, South Andaman, Koh Tao.

Scientific name:
"Coral Reefs" is the generic name for scores of individual coral species.

Life expectancy:
While individual polyps do not survive long, The colony can continue propagating for centuries.

Strange but true:
Coral reefs are not made up of plants but tiny animals called polyps.

Endangered?
Under threat from global and local problems (e.g. climate change and dynamite fishing)

Edible?
No

HARLEQUIN SHRIMP:
GHOST IN THE SHELL

A remarkable underwater renewal

The circle of life has some unique manifestations in Thailand's oceans. Among the thousands of species that inhabit Thai waters, there is a perpetual, dynamic cycle of change going on as each creature grows, evolves and eventually dies. Some fish change colour completely as they mature – like the juvenile emperor angelfish on page 43 – but harlequin shrimps have a way of renewing themselves that is truly spectacular.

Harlequin shrimp are remarkable enough for their super-vivid white and orange colours and paddle-like front legs. These tiny creatures, no more than a few centimetres long, look like they're dressed to go to the disco. Despite their loud clothing, they are extremely hard to find, preferring to remain deep inside a reef's crevices.

What's even more rare, however, is to witness the event caught in these photos at Koh Haa in the southern Andaman sea – the harlequin shrimp "moulting", leaving behind a ghostly replica of its former skin. In order to emerge from its old skin, the harlequin shrimp begins to shake and the front half, which covers its carapace, breaks off as it wriggles out of it, followed by the back end. The end result is a transparent carbon copy of the harlequin shrimp's shape that retains every curve and line of its creator.

Even more remarkably, this isn't a one-off, life-changing event: the harlequin shrimp sheds its skin every 18 days. And if performed by a female, it's considered a form of foreplay to its mating ritual with the male – a kind of striptease from its disco clothes.

Suitably renewed, the harlequin shrimp discards its ghostly shell and returns to hunting and mating – until the process begins again a few weeks later.

Left, above & below: Wrestling with myself: The harlequin shrimp begins to shake off the transparent husk of the exoskeleton.
Previous page: Mirror image: A harlequin shrimp sits next to the ghostly exoskeleton it has just discarded.
Next page: Getting ahead: With a final flourish, the shrimp's head emerges from the exoskeleton and its old ghostly-looking shell is discarded.

Left: Shiny and new: Finally free of its old exoskeleton, the harlequin shrimp can rejoin its mate, until the process starts again the following month.

BEYOND THE TSUNAMI

How one Thai island restored its devastated reefs

The tsunami of December 2004 was one of the worst natural disasters in history, causing widespread destruction in numerous countries along the Asian, Indian and African coasts. Thailand suffered considerable damage on its west coast, with Khao Lak, Phuket, Koh Phi Phi all badly affected, although other islands like Koh Lanta emerged relatively unscathed. Six years on, it's hard to imagine the tsunami ever happened – Thailand's west coast has rebuilt itself and tourists have returned, but there are valuable lessons to be learnt from the tsunami's terrible legacy.

Koh Phi Phi was one of the areas in Thailand worst affected by the tsunami. The scenic island set in the Andaman Sea off the coast of southern Thailand had long been popular with backpackers and scuba divers alike as an ocean paradise. Its reputation was sealed when it was chosen as the location for *The Beach*, the 2000 Hollywood movie that starred Leonardo DiCaprio. When the wave hit, it destroyed 60 percent of the buildings on the island and claimed nearly 1,300 lives. Many thought Phi Phi would never recover from the devastation wrought upon it by the sea, both on land and on its surrounding reefs. But throughout 2005, a truly Herculean clean-up effort carried out by Thai and tourist volunteers ensured that Phi Phi not only reopened for business, but that it was just as beautiful a place to visit and to dive.

Koh Phi Phi's reef cleanup was a huge logistical operation that went on for almost the entire year with the help of literally thousands of volunteers – divers and non-divers alike. Some 280 tonnes of debris were cleared from under the water and on the beaches. The debris retrieved from the water ranged from trees and construction materials (including a seven-tonne roof in one case) to personal effects vital in help-

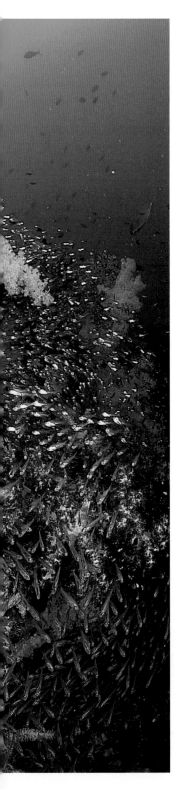

Left: The initial fear after the tsunami had struck was that the delicate, decades-old structure of Thailand's coral reefs had been decimated. Thankfully there were only a couple of dive sites that were severely damaged, with the rest soon recovering to pre-tsunami health.
Previous page: The debris of a dive shop destroyed by the 2004 tsunami on the island of Koh Lanta. Virtually all of Thailand's west coast was damaged by the giant wave, but has subsequently been wholly restored.

ing identify those missing in the wake of the disaster.

One of the key figures leading the cleanup operation was Andrew Hewett, a long-term Phi Phi resident and dive instructor who narrowly escaped the tsunami with his wife and children. As the project coordinator of Phi Phi Dive Camp, which was founded in February 2005 to formalise the reef restoration operations on the island, Hewett watched the cleanup grow from a seemingly impossible idea into an extraordinary achievement.

"The big surprise," says Hewett, "was that we actually achieved the goal of what we wanted to do when we started. Over the first six-month period, we averaged about 60 volunteers a day. The Dive Camp also employed up to 25 local Thai residents to help with the effort. In total, we had about 4,500 people assisting us. Volunteers included experienced divers, snorkellers, beach cleanup crews, boat crews, and other surface support teams. Approximately 7,500 dives were made to clear the debris."

At the same time, a number of other private groups helped to support the local community. Among these was the Hi Phi Phi group organised by Bang La and Claire West, who did a superb job of organising volunteers to help clean the streets and assist businesses to reopen. *Time Asia* named Hi Phi Phi as one of its Asia Heroes of 2005 for their efforts.

Both the Phi Phi Dive Camp and Hi Phi Phi organisations used their websites to attract more volunteers and to highlight the plight of the island. PADI (the Professional Association of Diving Instructors) publicised the Camp's dive operations on their online message boards, which brought in hundreds of divers from all over the world.

Once the bulk of the cleanup operation was complete, the Dive Camp disbanded into several ongoing projects, among them artificial reef and coral reef nursery constructions. These are both vital not only for cultivating Phi Phi's corals but also for educating the many tourists who have made Phi Phi one of Thailand's most popular places to visit since the tsunami.

The island itself has returned to its former state as well, with most businesses rebuilt and the environmental pressure of too many tourists already becoming a question mark over Koh Phi Phi once again. How Koh Phi Phi copes with its popularity in the future after surviving the tsunami remains to be seen.

© Photo by Ayesha Cantrell

USS LAGARTO

The incredible discovery of the lost American WWII submarine in Thailand's waters

On 3 May 1945, the American submarine *USS Lagarto* met with the *USS Baya* in the Gulf of Thailand to take on supplies. The war in Europe was only days away from ending, but in the Pacific it continued to rage on. After transferring the supplies, the two ships separated, agreeing to stay in radio contact. But the *Lagarto* and its crew of 86 submariners were never seen or heard from again.

It was not until sixty years later, almost to the day it disappeared, that the *Lagarto* was finally found – 70m down in the Gulf, far below the depth to which most scuba divers can dive – by two British wreck divers.

Jamie MacLeod and Stewart Oehl had sunk their life savings into buying their own boat, the *MV Trident*, to pursue their dream of deep wreck diving from their base on Koh Tao. They had deliberately set out to look for the *Lagarto*, working out an ocean floor survey plan from the last place where the submarine had been seen. Both assumed it would take them several years to find the *Lagarto*, but they had a spectacular stroke of luck.

Thai fishermen can occasionally be persuaded to part with the GPS marks of the best fishing grounds to be found – and as fish congregate around wrecks, this can lead divers to wholly undiscovered ships on the seabed.

As Stewart had acquired a new set of marks for 500 baht, Jamie drew the short straw of having to be the first one to go down and see what was there. There's no guarantee that checking a virgin set of marks will produce something interesting. It could be a pile of stones or debris or, more dangerously, a submerged pinnacle covered in lost fishing nets which can ensnare and trap an unwary diver.

"I followed the shot line down to 70m," recalls Jamie, "and suddenly, I realised that the line had landed just in front of the bow, so when you get to the bottom, you're right in front of the bow and looking up at it. It's unmistakable. The *Lagarto* was sitting upright on the bottom and it's like it's coming

© Photo by Ayesha Cantrell

Above: The USS Lagarto's starboard tube is open, indicating she fired a torpedo in her last moments.
Right: A fearsome 5-inch deck gun still stands guard on the Lagarto.
Previous page: Seventy metres down, a diver shines his torch on the submerge holes which finally identified this submarine wreck as the USS Lagarto.

© Photo by Ayesha Cantrell

© Photo by Ayesha Cantrell

straight towards you. You'll never forget it."

"It was the best 500 baht I had ever spent," Stewart says with a laugh.

Because the *Lagarto* is a war grave, Jamie and Stewart had contacted the United States Submarine Veterans of WWII Association before their quest for permission to search for the submarine and to keep them aware of their ongoing efforts. When they broke the news that they had found the *Lagarto*, the US Navy sent a team on the *USS Salvor* to verify the wreck themselves.

It was to be another two remarkable divers – Richie Kohler and John Chatterton – who would document the sunken submarine, providing definitive evidence that the *Lagarto* had been sunk by a depth charge dropped by the Japanese minesweeper *Hatsutaka*.

"I was hired by the Wisconsin Maritime Museum along with John Chatterton to do photo-documentary evidence of the wreck, having documented submarine wrecks before," explains Kohler. "We can apply a forensic approach looking at it. We're technical divers, deep divers with an expertise in shipwrecks. We were shooting high-definition movie footage using rebreather technology which allowed us to stay underwater for 3 hours at a time."

Chatterton and Kohler's previous experience documenting submarine wrecks was already the stuff of legend, thanks to Robert Kurson's bestselling book, *Shadow Divers*. The book documented the duo's six-year quest to identify a German U-Boat and its crew after it was inexplicably discovered off the New Jersey coast. *Shadow Divers* gained a huge audience because it dealt not only with high-adrenaline deep diving, but also with the history and human drama of trying to understand the events that had led to the U-Boat's demise. It also gave the families of the dead crew closure.

© Photo by Ayesha Cantrell

Left: The USS Lagarto's gun sight. **Above:** The USS Lagarto's target data transmitter, located at the conning tower, was used to sight targets and send coordinates to torpedoes.

Kohler learnt about the *Lagarto* while on a *Shadow Divers* book tour. "An older woman came over to me and said she was especially touched by the story," he explains. "Her father had been lost on an American submarine in the Gulf of Thailand and she wished that somebody would tell her what had happened to him. Almost a year after that, she emailed me this amazing story about how her dad's submarine had been discovered by two British divers."

Sparked by this news, and driven by his fascination with the history and mystery of lost ships, Kohler travelled halfway round the world from his native New Jersey in 2007 to dive the *Lagarto*, to honour the crew of the lost sub and analyse how it met its fate.

For the hardy few like Kohler and Chatterton, deep diving is a way of life, with all the rigorous training, special equipment and danger that it entails.

In this particular assignment, though, there was also a vital task Kohler had to carry out on his first dive to the *Lagarto*: "As I was heading out to Thailand I received a phone call from Nancy Kenney. Her father died on the *Lagarto* when she was three years old – she had nothing to know him by but the black-and-white photos she had of him. She knew that the diving was very dangerous and we would be filming the documentary. What she wanted me to do was rap on the side of the hull and say to her dad that she and her mum were okay and that they loved him very much. And that I did for Nancy."

After the flurry of international publicity that surrounded the *Lagarto*'s discovery, the submarine has been left in peace. Only Jamie, Stewart and the US Navy know the exact location of the *Lagarto*, and there will only be the occasional custodial dive on her in the future. She and her crew can now finally rest in peace.

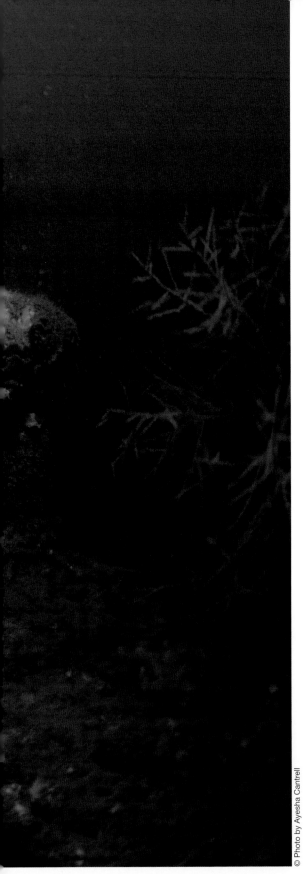

© Photo by Ayesha Cantrell

© Photo by Ayesha Cantrell

Above: A diver provides a sense of scale against the huge size of one of the USS Lagarto's twin propellers.
Left: Torchlight reveals the memorial plaque placed by the US Navy to honour the 86 sailors who lost their lives when the USS Lagarto sank. The plaque reads: "In memory of the fighting men in USS Lagarto (SS-371) from the crew of USS Salvor (ARS-51) 16 June 2006."

LEARNING TO DIVE

Get a lifelong passport into the underwater world

Thailand is one of the most popular places in the world to learn to scuba dive, and it's easy to see why – the combination of warm, blue waters with generally great visibility, affordable prices that are unrivalled by most other destinations, a mature scuba diving industry with hundreds of certified operators to choose from, and Thailand's own unique charm above and below water make it hard to beat. Indeed, it's become something of a rite of passage for many backpackers to get their scuba certification when travelling in Thailand, as there are few other places which offer so much value. Thailand's dive industry is effectively geared towards introducing new people to scuba diving, and therefore it's possible for new divers to easily get individual tuition or any other special requests as required.

GETTING YOUR CERTIFICATE
Learning to dive in Thailand typically takes three or four days. PADI (Professional Association of Dive Instructors) and SSI (Scuba

Schools International) are the two main certification agencies in Thailand, and a certification card from either agency means a newly certified diver can dive anywhere in the world as both agencies are widely recognised, with PADI currently the world's largest dive agency. Both organisations stress safety first at all points of learning, and their teaching programme has been constantly refined to ensure students are never at risk while learning to dive. In fact, compared to other adventure sports, diving has one of the most rigorous sets of safety procedures possible.

After signing up for an Open Water Diver course with a dive shop, a new diver is shown a couple of training videos to familiarise him with the concepts and skills involved in diving. This is usually done on the evening before Day One proper of the dive course. On the morning of Day One, it's straight into the swimming pool to try on the scuba gear and to get used to the strange concept of breathing underwater. After a couple of hours of learning the skills to move around under-

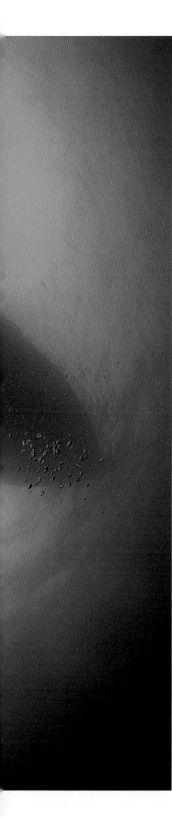

Left: Everything takes on a different perspective underwater, including seeing the boat from beneath.
Previous page: Backward rolling into the water from a boat commando-style is one of the techniques taught when learning to dive.

water, there's lunch followed by a couple of hours' theory to explain how diving works and the important dive safety concepts. Teaching regulations stipulate that there can be no more than eight students to one diving instructor, and most dive shops usually work with a maximum of six.

On Day Two, there is a session of theory before the first real dives in the ocean. The dives are done in shallow areas and involve learning more skills underwater before going to explore the reef itself. Day Three sees two more dives in the ocean and a final theory session before the presentation of scuba certification cards, after which each student is acknowledged as a full-fledged scuba diver able to continue to explore Thailand's underwater world.

TYPES OF COURSES

The Open Water Course in Thailand can be taken while one is based at a guesthouse or resort, or on a live-aboard boat. If the former, day-trips are made over the three-day course, with a total of four dives, and students return to their resort each evening. If the course is taken on a live-aboard boat, which typically spends four days at sea, the divers get to do a total of 13 dives, including the four from their dive course. The resort and day-trip option is available everywhere – Koh Tao, Koh Phi Phi, Koh Lanta and Phuket are the most popular options as bases for day-trip diving. Thailand live-aboards go to the Similan Islands (see page 184) or Southern Andaman region (see page 186). Live-aboards depart from Khao Lak, Phuket and Koh Lanta.

Koh Tao is the undisputed king when it comes to learning to dive on a budget in Thailand, and dive shops there offer discounted accommodation as a matter of course for those who sign up for their dive courses. There are dive schools that cater to literally hundreds of divers and smaller operations that focus on personal service and individual tuition.

Learning to dive on a Thailand live-aboard boat is more expensive, but it offers many more dives so that new divers can reinforce their new skills and continue diving with their instructor beyond the course itself. By continuing to dive immediately after getting certified, new divers refine their skills and will become even more relaxed and accustomed to being underwater.

For those who simply wish to give diving a try without committing to the full multi-day course, trial dives are available where you get to scuba dive in the ocean under the supervision and instruction of a scuba instructor.

SNORKELLING AND FREEDIVING

Scuba gear isn't necessary to explore Thailand's oceans

You don't need to be a scuba diver to explore Thailand's underwater world. Snorkelling is a fun, easy and very cheap way of taking to the water and seeing for yourself what lies in the Thai seas. Thailand's usually calm sea conditions make it an ideal place to try snorkelling. With a mask providing a view of what lies below and a snorkel making breathing effortless, a snorkeller can simply relax and float on the ocean, enjoying the corals and fish life dappling in the sunlight. It's a fantastic way to introduce both kids and adults to the sea and to motivate them to practise swimming and so become more confident in the water.

Masks, snorkels and fins for hire are ubiquitous in Thailand, and the benign weather conditions mean that one can get started on snorkelling by simply walking straight into the water at most Thai beaches. Not all beaches have good coral and fish life, however – a dedicated snorkelling daytrip is the best way to see the best reefs

for snorkelling. It's important to check with the locals first about what to watch out for when entering water from the shore – for example, riptides – and to wear a life vest if you are not a strong swimmer. Waterproof sunscreen is also essential.

Snorkellers in Thailand can quite often see turtles coming to the surface for air, octopuses drifting across the reef, and lots of different tropical fish – from clownfish to parrotfish and anthias. If exploring out at the Similan Islands, snorkellers may encounter a majestic manta ray. Those with incredible luck may even see a whale shark at the surface, but that's a very rare event.

SNORKELLING HOTSPOTS

Among Thailand's snorkelling hotspots on the east coast is Koh Nangyuan, a small island that's next to Koh Tao and just a few minutes' boat ride away. It has several shallow coral gardens to explore. Over on Koh Tao itself, Shark Bay has long been a favou-

Above: A snorkel makes it effortless to simply relax and float on the surface of the ocean.
Left: The mermaid-like monofin lets freedivers explore the ocean on a single breath of air without any need for scuba gear.
Previous page: Snorkelling is the easiest and cheapest way to get up close and personal with the amazing marine life of Thailand's oceans.

rite as it's both a beautiful small beach and a place where it's possible to see baby black-tip sharks, as the bay is their nursery. Ao Leuk and Ao Laem Thian also offer interesting corals to explore but a bit of a bike ride is required to access these two bays by land.

On the west coast, Koh Kradan and Koh Rok are two small islands with lush corals and good visibility. Both are accessible by day-trips from Koh Lanta. Koh Lipe, right at the southern tip of Thailand on the Malaysian border, also has beautiful reefs on some of its small adjoining islands.

For hardcore snorkellers, probably the best way to see some of Thailand's fantastic reefs and perhaps meet a manta ray on the surface is to take a dedicated snorkelling trip to the Similan Islands. This experience includes staying on a boat for a couple of nights so as to fully explore the islands. The Surin Islands, which lie to the north of the

Similan Islands, are also considered a great snorkelling destination but require a fairly long boat trip to get to.

FREEDIVING
Another way to explore Thailand's oceans unencumbered by scuba gear is freediving. It is the nearest that a human can get to experiencing the ocean unmediated. This art of holding one's breath long enough to easily descend to depths of 30m or more allows a closer interaction with marine life because there's no noise and bubbles from scuba gear to scare them away. With a few simple techniques, it is quite easy to breath-hold for a couple of minutes. Freediving was once considered a sporting discipline that was the preserve of only the super-fit, but it is actually easily accessible to everyone, whatever the fitness level and age.

FEAR FACTOR

Dangerous Creatures To Watch Out For

Sharks may not be the dangerous menace they've been made out to be in Thailand's waters, but there are other denizens of Thai seas that anyone entering the water should watch out for. A sense of perspective needs to be kept about these creatures – snorkellers and divers are far more likely to injure themselves bumping against coral, which may look soft but can be very sharp and can also sting. The advice to only look and don't touch is particularly important when entering the ocean. None of these creatures will attack unless they are provoked, or accidentally touched or trodden on.

STONEFISH

Stonefish are remarkably ugly, squat fish that position themselves in the reef and change colour to blend in with their surroundings. They are officially the most venomous fish in the world, delivering neurotoxins through the spines on their backs. These spines are raised when they feel threatened and the toxin is venomous enough to kill a human being. Incidents involving stonefish are usu-ally due to people standing on them thinking they are stones. The pain from a stonefish sting can be eased by hot water but an anti-venom is often required to fully counter it.

SCORPIONFISH

Scorpionfish have the same camouflage techniques as stonefish but they are somewhat smaller and more colourful in their mottled livery. They too have extremely poisonous spines on their back and usually spend their time waiting motionless for prey on the reef.

LIONFISH

Lionfish are technically part of the scorpionfish family, but their delicate spines and stunning markings – typically white and black stripes or a crimson red – tend to distract from the fact that they also possess highly venomous spines. Lionfish are extremely common on the west coast of Thailand and tend to congregate in groups, drifting slowly with the current while waiting to ambush their next meal. They usually move very slowly and so can be easily avoided.

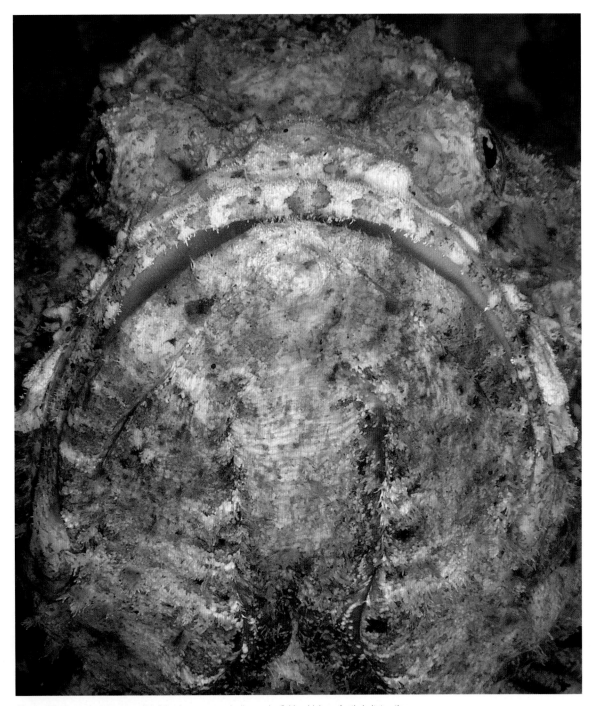

Above: The face of a false stonefish (also known as a devil scorpionfish), which perfectly imitates the seabed's rocks, and has highly poisonous spines on its back.

Left: With their sharp teeth and powerful jaws, moray eels can inflict vicious wounds if threatened or goaded by divers. However, they are usually placid if left well alone.

Previous page: One of the most beautiful but deadly fish in Thailand's oceans, the lionfish has extremely potent toxins in its dorsal spines which can administer an extremely painful sting.

Left: Like the stonefish, scorpionfish are so well disguised on the reef as to be near invisible. If accidentally touched, they can deliver a painful sting through their dorsal spines.

MORAY EELS

Moray eels are fearsome-looking, growing up to 3 metres in length. Their powerful jaws and sharp teeth can inflict severe wounds on anyone foolish enough to put their hands into their reef homes, but otherwise they tend to be peaceable despite their dragon-like appearance.

SEA SNAKES

Sea snakes perhaps inspire the most fear when they're seen underwater, thanks to people's general apprehension of snakes. The banded sea snake is spotted fairly often on both coasts of Thailand and is extremely venomous. However, there are no records of attacks on divers or snorkellers. Sea snakes tend to be curious but not aggressive – they are quite docile, in fact – and their mouth is small, which makes it difficult for them to get a bite to inject their venom.

CROWN-OF-THORNS STARFISH

The velvet-looking body of the crown-of-thorns starfish is covered in sharp spikes. It's not only toxic to human touch but also to the coral reef itself. Wherever the crown-of-thorns goes, it leaves behind a trail of destruction as it voraciously feeds on the reef. The giant triton, its natural predator, has declined in numbers because of demand for its conch shell. This has left the crown-of-thorns to breed almost unchecked. Only the plucky harlequin shrimp (see page 136) will attack and feed on the crown-of-thorns. Some conservationists argue that the crown-of-thorns starfish need human intervention to physically stop them from destroying reefs. Previous tactics to remove them were unsuccessful because it was found that starfish regenerated when cut up by divers – each severed piece grew into a new crown-of-thorns. Others think this is part of the natural, decades-long cycle of the reef's lifetime and they should be left alone.

CONE SNAILS

Cone snails are perhaps the most innocuous of Thailand's harmful sea creatures. Their exquisite, elegant, tapered shells invite closer inspection and handling – but doing so can result in an extremely painful surprise. The snail has a harpoon that it uses to attack its usually faster-moving prey from a distance. This shoots out of the cone armed with a potent neurotoxin. There have been confirmed fatalities worldwide that are ascribed to certain species of cone snails – including the *Conus textile*, which is found in Thailand – underlining the point that one should never touch anything while in the water.

Left & above: Despite being greatly feared and very poisonous, sea snakes are curious rather than aggressive around divers. Watching them sidewind across the reef and head to the surface for air is quite mesmerising.

Above: This beautiful cone shell has a literal sting in the tail – a poison dart can emerge through the top of the shell if handled by unwitting humans, delivering a potentially lethal injection of venom.

Left: Besides administering a toxic sting to anyone who touches it, the rapidly reproducing crown-of-thorns starfish is widely regarded as being responsible for destroying large swathes of coral reef.

THE FUTURE OF THAILAND'S UNDERWATER WORLD

Will Thailand's marine life survive the 21st century

What does the future hold for the amazing biodiversity of Thailand's oceans? Virtually every chapter in this book has touched on the very real threats to the well-being of individual marine species like sharks, turtles and manta rays in Thailand, and the more far-reaching concerns about the health of Thailand's reefs and fish stocks in general.

Although mass tourism came to Thailand only in the last 40 years, and Thailand's scuba diving industry developed into a multi-million dollar industry at the same time, there's no doubt that tourism has had an adverse impact on some of Thailand's aquatic environments. The generations that have been lucky enough to see Thailand's reefs and marine life thanks to advances in travel and technology might be the last generations to see them anywhere near their full health, as celebrated by Jacques Cousteau and others.

TAKING ACTION

It's important that people continue to carry out conservation work in their own aquatic backyards because they are, in a sense, pioneering the rescue and replenishment of the reefs. Commendable initiatives include Biorock Thailand, which attempts to stimulate coral growth, along with the building of artificial reefs to provide habitats for fish life, and clownfish releases on Koh Lanta and Pattaya to boost local reef population.

Public education on valuing the reefs and not damaging them, and the enforcement of proper controls over the number of reef visitors allowed into any one area – Koh Phi Phi is a salient example – are local solutions that can be easily implemented. Development and pollution controls can also be enforced in Thailand if given the political will and sufficient resources; but

Left and previous page: Thailand's corals, like the rest of the world's, consume the carbon dioxide that humans create. But there is a limit to how much the reefs can take, and the saturation point may be near.

many of the problems that Thailand's marine habitat faces are international rather than local, and require rapid international co-operation if the reefs are to survive. Governments need to recognise that, at the international level, concerted action has to be taken very quickly and that drastic measures are required to reduce the amount of carbon dioxide emission and over-fishing and to address the world's booming population.

Without this sort of action, the good work carried out by people like Andrew Hewett on Koh Phi Phi (see page 147) becomes all the more difficult – individuals can make local change, but only governments can enact and enforce sweeping national and international legislation required to make a lasting improvement.

NO FISH, NO FOOD
Because the reefs are underwater, they are out of sight and out of mind for most people – and were they to disappear, only relatively few people would initially notice. If the reefs are allowed to continue to deteriorate, it would begin to have a tangible

impact on everyday life for many people – both in the increase in air pollution due to more carbon dioxide being in the air, to the collapse of fish stocks, a problem that has already affected the UK and Europe with the virtual disappearance of cod – once a staple. More and more fish species will disappear, and food for humans will become scarcer if industrial methods of fishing, which take far more than required and regularly destroy the reef environment with it, are allowed to continue.

A CURE FOR CANCER?
The reef is a vast resource that has only just begun to be understood and used. Thailand's reefs have contributed to the creation of numerous medicines which use the properties of particular species to synthesise new treatments. For example, the poisonous cone snail (see page 169) has been used to create a painkiller, and there are other medicines for AIDS, cancer and asthma, among others, that are based on reef organisms. Compared to the billions of dollars devoted to exploring outer space, the allocation of international funds

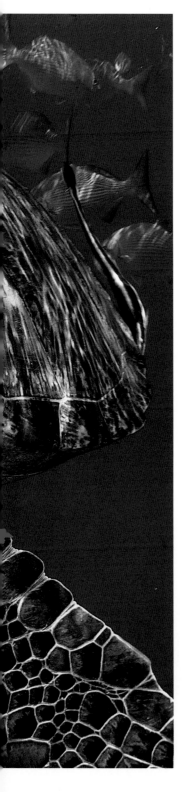

Below: Because of their beauty, ghost pipefish are often hunted for the aquarium trade, despite being extremely difficult to keep alive in captivity.
Left: Once plentiful in Thailand's waters, the country's turtles have plunged dramatically in number over the last few decades.

to research the inner space of the world's oceans is tiny – only around 10 percent of it has been fully explored and mapped. Even creatures that are fairly regularly encountered in Thai waters, like the manta ray, the whale shark, and even the frogfish, are still largely mysterious – little is known for certain about them, and research continually brings new surprises.

IT'S NOT TOO LATE

The potential for new discoveries and harnessing the power of the reefs to help sustain future generations of the world's population is almost limitless if the current problems of global warming, pollution and over-fishing can be addressed and the reefs preserved and replenished. It is true that

the prognosis for Thailand's reefs, like for those around the world, is quite grim – the more pessimistic have even argued that it might be already too late and that we have gone beyond the point of no return. Coral bleaching, where the coral turns white due to stress brought about by the water temperature being too warm, has begun to affect Thailand's reefs in some areas.

But it is precisely because we know relatively little about the reefs that there is still hope – coral life often astounds scientists with the rapid regeneration it can make in the wake of isolated natural and man-made disasters. There is only hope, however, if the threat to the reefs is fully acknowledged and decisive action is taken to preserve the wonders of Thailand's underwater world.

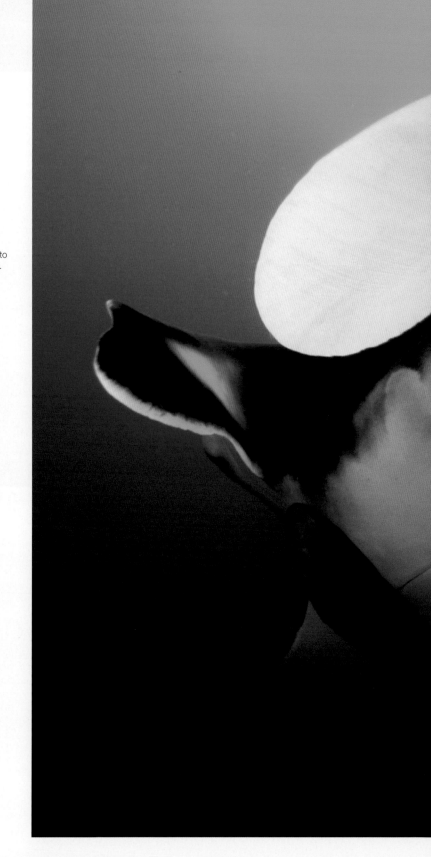

Right: Despite their size, manta rays are vulnerable to fishermen and are increasingly hunted for their meat.

Left: Until there is a concerted international effort to protect the whale shark, these gentle giants will continue to be hunted for their fins and meat until, most likely, extinction.

SIMILAN ISLANDS

Above: The Similan Islands are famed for their beauty both above and below water.

Universally considered Thailand's best diving destination, the Similan Islands (Koh Similan) are a group of nine islands in the Andaman Sea off Thailand's west coast. The islands are about 65 km from the town of Khao Lak on the mainland and 90 km from Phuket. Combining a collection of dive sites that provide a smorgasbord of marine life sightings both big and small, as well as excellent visibility and flat, calm ocean conditions, the Similan Islands are popular for value-priced live-aboard trips. It's possible to do speedboat day-trips from Khao Lak too, but the long, bumpy ride there and back is not the most pleasant way to experience the diving.

Similan live-aboard trips usually take in the nine islands of the Similans themselves as well as three sites

outside the Similan marine park – Koh Bon, Koh Tachai and Richelieu Rock. Undoubtedly Thailand's best overall live-aboard experience, the sheer variety of the Similans' dive sites and marine life will keep divers of all experience levels happy.

East of Eden

A dream site for underwater photographers, East of Eden is an easily navigable, gently sloping coral reef that goes down to around 35m. The unarguable highlight of this site is the huge bommie within the reef – some 12m tall, resplendent with a technicolor riot of coral, and hordes of fish moving in and out of it. It's difficult to decide where to look first. Leopard sharks can be found down at 35m, lying on the sandy bottom.

What you might see: Leopard sharks, cuttlefish, blackjack, trevally, stonefish, octopuses, fusiliers and snappers.

North Point

A collection of huge boulders on the slope of Similan Island Number 9 constitute this dive site, providing a collection of great swim-throughs and hiding places for fish life. Currents can be strong but the rocks provide shelter. Reef sharks and leopard sharks are often found at 35m, languidly sitting on the sand. Turtles are also seen at this site, as they enjoy munching the coral which sits on the slope's expansive plateau at around 7m.

What you might see: Leopard sharks, turtles, boxfish, octopuses.

Koh Bon

A very distinctive site, with a sheer drop of granite that plunges vertically from the surface to around 25m before levelling out. With good visibility, you can see the wall stretch away beside and beneath you, creating a distinct flying sensation. Manta rays frequently come to Koh Bon and cruise the length of the wall – unsurprisingly, they are the star attraction of this site. There are numerous creatures living in the crevices of the wall such as moray eels, and night dives here reveal beautiful creatures like the white banded boxer shrimp.

What you might see: Manta rays, leopard sharks, octopuses, blacktip sharks, moray eels.

Richelieu Rock

A stunning horseshoe-shaped pinnacle in the ocean, Richelieu Rock is home to an abundance of marine life that uses it as a shelter and a hunting ground. The density of fish life here is astounding – descending the line can be a little tricky because of the sheer number of glassfish all around you! Seahorses live at the end of one of the Rock's prongs, at about 35m, with frogfish and stone-

fish nestled in the rocks. Currents can be strong but the inside of the horseshoe provides shelter with a depth of about 11m. Whale sharks frequently visit, and while their presence cannot be guaranteed, there is more than enough at Richelieu to keep divers occupied.

What you might see: Whale sharks, barracuda, frogfish, stonefish, seahorses, numerous fish species

Best time to go diving

The Similan Islands are only open from November to April each year. They are closed from May to September because conditions are too rough for safe diving in the monsoon season. Some live-aboard boats get a special dispensation to begin trips in the last two weeks of October.

SOUTHERN ANDAMAN

Above: The stunning limestone karsts of Koh Phi Phi.

Phuket, Koh Phi Phi and Koh Lanta are not as well-known as the Similans but are, at their best, comparable in the quality of their marine life and the visibility of their waters.

Phuket is Thailand's most visited island and also the most well-developed; from humble backpacker origins, it has gone decidedly upmarket, with luxury villas and hotels throughout the island. Koh Phi Phi, made famous by the movie *The Beach*, is also one of the most popular islands to visit in Thailand, especially for backpackers. Koh Lanta, by contrast, is very laid-back and considered quite sleepy, despite its rising popularity; it is geographically best situated for day-trips to the main South Andaman dive sites.

Hin Daeng / Hin Muang

These two ocean pinnacles provide dramatic dive sites, sloping down to 60m. Currents can be strong and visibility sometimes poor – but these are more than made up for by the manta rays that use the pinnacles as a cleaning station. Several mantas can be seen here at any one time, circling the rock, seemingly unperturbed by divers. On the days that they're not around, there are plenty of other creatures that can be spotted.

What you might see: Manta rays, groupers, leopard sharks, cuttlefish, octopuses.

Koh Bida

Koh Bida actually comprises two islands – Bida Nok and Bida Yai – with several dive sites located on their underwater slopes. Koh Bida has variable conditions, with poor visibility on some occasions, but it's a great site for seeing coral and marine life. Beautifully coloured nudibranchs and seahorses live along Bida's wall, which goes down to around 28m, but there are also plenty of shallow areas too.

Above: Koh Haa's five towering rocks provide sanctuary in the middle of the ocean.

What you might see: Nudibranchs, turtles, seahorses.

Koh Haa

A circle of five small granite islands, Koh Haa has numerous dive sites which all enjoy spectacular visibility and some great marine life. Wall dives outside the rocks yield huge schools of barracuda hanging in the blue, octopuses moving along the coral and seahorses at 35m, waiting in the archway of a dramatic swim-through. Koh Haa Yai has a beautiful chimney ascent, where you can slowly come up within the rock itself and reach the air pocket at the top of the cave. Within the shallow lagoon formed by the five islands, there are numerous macro delights, including the harlequin shrimp and ghost pipefish.

What you might see: Barracuda, octopuses, reef sharks, seahorses, nudibranchs, harlequin shrimps, ghost pipefish, cuttlefish.

Best time to go diving

November to April is the best time to dive the aman sites. The monsoon season from May to October makes these sites inaccessible from time to time due to the rough seas. Koh Phi Phi and Phuket have sheltered reefs nearby that can be dived all year round.

Koh Phi Phi

Koh Bida

Koh Lanta

Koh Haa

Hin Muang

Hin Daeng

KOH TAO

Above: Koh Tao's quiet bays provide a nursery for local marine life.

You might find it hard to locate Koh Tao on a map of Thailand; until recently, this tiny speck of an island in the Gulf of Thailand was often missed by cartographers. For such a small place, Koh Tao now has a big reputation – besides Cairns in Australia, it's now the biggest place to learn to scuba dive in all of the Asia-Pacific, with over 40,000 new divers being certified on the island each year.

With this growth in popularity, Koh Tao has transformed from an obscure and remote island with only basic facilities for hardcore divers into a burgeoning dive industry geared to beginners, along with a laid-back but vibrant night-life scene. Accommodation and eateries have similarly blossomed so that it's possible to get pretty much any major cuisine on the island, and stay in digs from humble beach huts to five-star boutique hotels.

Despite its discovery by tourists, Koh Tao still remains a small and somewhat sleepy island, particularly when compared to neighbouring Koh Samui and Koh Phangan. There're no skyscraper hotels on Koh Tao, nor any international junk food and coffee shops. There's no airport either – and it's unlikely that one will ever be built on its steep jungle hillsides – so it requires several hours on a ferry to get there. This fact alone provides a natural throttle on the number of visitors coming to Koh Tao and helps preserve its chilled-out charm.

Close to Koh Tao lies the Ang Thong Marine Park,

reportedly the inspiration for Alex Garland's bestselling novel, *The Beach* (even though the movie was filmed at Koh Phi Phi). Ang Thong, as well as the main Koh Tao sites, is where occasional special live-aboard trips tend to explore.

Technical Diving

Koh Tao also has a burgeoning technical diving scene for experienced divers who want to take on the challenge of going deeper – the numerous deepwater wrecks within the Gulf of Thailand and relatively benign conditions make it an ideal place to learn technical diving skills.

Live-aboards and Day-trips

There are no regularly scheduled live-aboards operating in the Koh Tao area – the vast majority of diving is done on day-trips from the island. (Email local dive shops for information on any upcoming special live-aboard trips.) Most Koh Tao dive boats are customised Thai fishing boats. It takes no more than half an hour to get to any of the major sites, except Sail Rock, which takes 2–3 hours. Day-trip boats typically depart in the early morning or early afternoon for two dives each trip. Every dive shop includes scuba-gear hire in the price and has staff that can also teach you to dive.

Chumphon Pinnacle

Starting at 16m and going down to 35m, the lozenge-shaped Chumphon Pinnacle is the finest dive site in the Gulf of Thailand. Batfish, large groupers, blue spotted stingrays, moray eels and a host of other creatures call the pinnacle their home, but the main attraction for most divers are the sizeable (2m and bigger) grey reef sharks which frequently pass by in packs, about 25m off the southwest tip of the pinnacle. Schools of barracuda also hang in the blue of the northern tip. Whale sharks arrive at the pinnacle a few times each year.

What you might see: Grey reef sharks, batfish, groupers, boxfish, whale sharks.

South West Pinnacle

A small mountain of a dive site, South West provides a great pinnacle to slowly circle, gradually moving towards its apex through the dive. Scattered around the base of the main pinnacle are a score of other smaller ones, at about 25m to 30m, providing a happy hunting ground for fish and divers alike. Clouds of glassfish hang on the main pinnacle proper, while a school of batfish perch at the top of the pinnacle 5m from the surface, to keep divers company during their safety stop. Whale sharks are also occasionally sighted here each year.

What you might see: Groupers, damselfish, snappers, barracuda, leopard sharks, whale sharks.

Sail Rock

A big pinnacle right in the middle of the ocean, Sail Rock is nearly 3 hours' cruise from Koh Tao and definitely a lot easier to get to from Koh Samui. The visibility out at the rock can be pretty awful but when the gods are smiling, it can be a magical dive. The focal point of any Sail Rock dive is The Chimney, an opening in the coral that begins at around 15m and lets the diver ascend inside the wall itself to emerge at 5m on. The chimney is just about big enough to allow two divers to go up together, but it's better to do so one at a time to avoid bashing any of the coral growing within the chimney's confines as well. Care needs to be taken not to ascend too fast.

What you might see: Blackjack fish, trevally, tuna, barracuda, leopard sharks, whale sharks.

Hin Daeng

Hin Daeng near Koh Tao – not to be confused with its pinnacle namesake in Southern Thailand – is one of the Gulf of Thailand's hidden delights. Ostensibly a sloping reef dive, Hin Daeng's coral has coalesced into colourful towers that make the reef look like an aquatic city. The coral merges together at its base and then the towers soar up to heights of six to ten feet. The reef fish and even occasional sea snakes love to pop in and out of the many nooks and crannies among the coral, adding to the feeling of passing over some sort of underwater metropolis. There is also an excellent U-shaped swim-through which filters light from above to remarkable effect on the fish hovering within the swim-through's confines.

What you might see: Turtles, sea snakes, groupers, parrotfish, banner fish.

Best time to go diving

March to August is the best time to go to Koh Tao as the monsoon season takes full effect from September to November with frequent heavy rain and rough seas. The monsoon dissipates in December through to February,

ELSEWHERE IN THAILAND

Krabi

Krabi's coastline on the Andaman coast is incredibly scenic, particularly at Railay Beach and Ao Nang, with a few local reefs for casual divers to explore. Dive boats here will also run out to Koh Bida and other dive sites located around Koh Phi Phi.

Koh Samui and Koh Phangan

Both popular tourist islands, Samui and Phangan are not particularly good for scuba diving – there are some local reefs, but operators on both islands tend to go by speedboat to the dive sites around Koh Tao. The main exception is Sail Rock, one of the Gulf of Thailand's best dive sites, as it's easier to go there from Koh Samui and Koh Phangan.

Koh Samui is Thailand's most popular tourist island after Phuket, and is now an increasingly upmarket destination, and becoming more and more developed. There's plenty of luxury here, as well as day-trip access by speedboat to the major sites of the Gulf of Thailand for divers who just want to do one or two dives.

Koh Phangan, famous for its monthly Full Moon parties, is a large island with distinctly more tranquil northern beaches. It's a good getaway for those looking for empty beaches and inexpensive health retreats. A few operators on the island will explore local reefs. You can also head to Koh Tao's main sites by speedboat from here.

But if you are looking to spend most of your holiday diving rather than a couple of fun dives, you're probably better off going straight to Koh Tao.

Koh Chang

Almost on the border with neighbouring Cambodia, Koh Chang is one of Thailand's newer island destinations that have seen increasing development over the last few years. The island has some fairly interesting reefs but visibility can be poor.

Pattaya

Pattaya, a bustling city which sits at the top of the Gulf of Thailand, is a must-see for wreck divers. There are three shipwrecks off Pattaya at recreational depths to explore – the *Kood*, the *Khram* and the *Hardeep* – along with several technical wreck dive sites below 40m.

Koh Lipe

A tiny island on the Thai–Malaysian border, Koh Lipe has the real Robinson Crusoe feel, although it is becoming increasingly popular. Diving here can be excellent but conditions are quite variable.

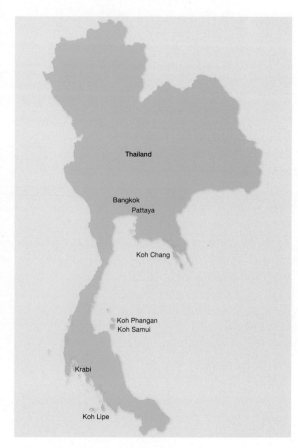

FURTHER READING & WEBSITES

Pocket Divesite: Similan
Pocket Divesite: South Andaman
by Polpich (Aey) Komson, Chutinun (Meen) Mora, Parnupong Norasethkamol, and Sesivie Pinyowit
(Vacation in Design, 2006)
www.pocketdivesite.com

Lonely Planet Diving and Snorkeling Thailand
by Tim Rock
(Lonely Planet)

Whale Sharks: The Giants of Ningaloo Reef
by Geoff Taylor
(HarperCollins, 1994)

Shark: The Shadow Below
by Hugh Edwards
(HarperCollins, 1998)

Nudibranchs Encyclopedia: Catalogue of
Asia/Indo-Pacific Sea Slugs
by Neville Coleman
(Neville Coleman's Underwater Geographic, 2008)

Reef Fish Identification: Tropical Pacific
by Gerald Allen et al
(New World Publications, 2003)

Asia Pacific Reef Guide
by Helmut Debelius
(Ikan Unterwasser-Archiv, 2001)

Thailand's Underwater World
www.thailandsunderwaterworld.com

Dive Guide Thailand
www.diveguidethailand.com

Scuba Diver AustralAsia
www.scubadiveraa.com

Asian Diver
www.asiandiver.com

Fins Online
www.finsonline.com

Scubaboard
www.scubaboard.com